The Writing Menu

Ensuring Success for Every Student

The Writing Menu
Ensuring Success for Every Student

Melissa Forney

MAUPIN HOUSE

The Writing Menu
Ensuring Success for Every Student

Editor: Candace Nelson
Cover: David Dishman
Book Designer: Melissa Forney
Graphics: Corel Mega Gallery © 1996

Library of Congress Cataloging-in-Publication Data

Forney, Melissa, 1952-
    The writing menu : ensuring success for every student / Melissa
Forney.
        p. cm.
    Includes bibliographical references (p.) and index.
    ISBN 0-929895-33-9
    1. English language—Composition and exercises—Study and teaching
(Elementary)—United States. 2. Creative Writing (Elementary
education)—United States. I. Title.
LB1576-F634   1999
372.62'3044—dc21   99-37476
                                                                      CIP

Other Professional Resources by Melissa Forney
        Dynamite Writing Ideas
        Razzle Dazzle Writing
        Oonawassee Summer
        To Shape a Life
        A Medal for Murphy

Melissa Forney is a writer, consultant, and keynote speaker. For booking information for
teacher seminars, young author conferences, or keynote speaking call 1-800-524-0634.

Maupin House publishes professional resources for innovative language arts teachers and
provides excellent inservice trainers, workshop presenters, and keynote speakers.

Maupin House

Maupin House Publishing, Inc.
PO Box 90148
Gainesville, FL 32607
1-800-524-0634
Fax: 352-373-5546
Email: info@maupinhouse.com
www.maupinhouse.com
10 9 8 7 6 5

For Aaron and Rebecca.
You are both so talented it scares me.

Contents

Acknowledgments

I'd like to thank the people who have made this book
possible with their editing, advice, or encouragement:
My editor, Julia Graddy, my mother, Jackie Forrest,
my mother-in-law, Charlotte Forney, and my friends,
Norma and Dan McCraw, Margaret Webb, Faye Settle, and
my colleague, Marcia Freeman. As always, a very special thanks
to my loving and supportive husband and best friend, Rick Forney.

CHAPTER ONE
Why Young Writers Need Writing Menus

Teaching kids to write should be a satisfying collaboration, not capital punishment. Self-expression should be a joy, not a chore. Writing can permeate every avenue of learning and unlock the interests, curiosity, and learning styles of each child. However, writing should be designed with individual differences in mind. When it comes to writing, there is no such thing as, "One size fits all."

Everyone loves choice. Teachers, kids, big folks, little folks. Choice is good. This book is based on the premise that when it comes to writing topics, genres, and projects, choice and variety are not only good, but vital keys to a child's education.

If you were raised on a steady diet of What I Did Over Summer Vacation, if you've ever read and graded 32 identical reports on sea mammals, if you've ever thought, "I'll die if I have to come up with another prompt," this book is for you.

Teaching writing and encouraging kids to write every single day both help to produce excellent writers. Sounds good in theory, doesn't it? Putting it into practice is a different story. The meltdown usually occurs somewhere between the beginning of the writing workshop and the Betty Ford Center.

You might need a little restructuring that will simplify your life and liberate your students. If you're ready for change in your classroom, ready to enhance your teaching style, ready to start a writing explosion, read on.

Teaching writing with writing menus will allow you to:

✳ Address multiple learning styles...
✳ Create enthusiasm for writing...
✳ Allow children freedom of choice...
✳ Propagate ongoing writing projects...
✳ Enable "ownership" and self-discipline...
✳ Establish independent learning...
✳ Spur lifelong writers...
✳ Raise writing assessment scores...
✳ Foster critical thinking, good choices, and value judgements...
✳ Encourage children to make good use of their time...
✳ Provide writing assignments for a multitude of attention spans...
✳ Help kids share knowledge with the class in many different ways...
✳ Foster a creative environment for writing workshops...

What is a writing menu, and how does it work?

The writing menu is exactly what the name suggests: a menu of writing topics, genres, and projects kids may choose from. The beauty is that menus provide a variety of choices that stem from and enhance topics you are currently teaching.

In a nutshell, the writing menu works like this. With each new unit of study, you provide a companion writing menu. During the writing workshop, students choose projects that appeal to them based on topic, genre, length of time, and interest.

The menus can be made ahead of time when you plan your units and can be put on computer disks so they can be used year after year. Teams or multi-age teachers might share menus. Each writing menu will be used for several weeks or the duration of the units you are studying. The option of points adds incentive.

During the daily writing workshop, students will write on projects selected from their menus. Once the writing menu has been activated, the idea is for kids to make wise, but independent, choices. This takes some training, but the results are well worth the effort. Kids may work on one or two lengthy projects, a variety of shorter assignments, or a combination of both. Points can be assigned to each project according to its difficulty. If they so choose, kids may work on writing and revision, illustrations, costumes, props, or additional projects at home. This doubles or triples time spent on writing and its enhancements.

The teacher's role is to facilitate, motivate, give personal help, troubleshoot, and encourage students to be productive and on task. The teacher also teaches individual writing skills or guided, layered revision at the beginning of each writing workshop. The writing menu workshop works best if the teacher is readily available as a manager and adviser.

At the end of the unit, teachers and students will together assess content, creativity, the skills and goals that have been accomplished, and a variety of other factors. Children will have the opportunity to present one or more of their writing projects to the class.

How does the writing menu differ from traditional writing assignments?

Traditionally, teachers have given the same writing assignment to an entire class. For instance, all children write reports on specific states. All children write a book report on a famous inventor. All children give speeches on the importance of democracy. Children are often given the same length of time to write and finish a project. When it is time to present their projects, the class (and the poor teacher!) has to sit through the monotonous litany of 30 reports or speeches.

Think about how *you* work on projects at *home*. Some of us are morning people, others aren't even human until afternoon. Some days you can hardly face your chores and other days you surprise yourself by cleaning that dreaded closet. Some people like long, satisfying projects; others like the satisfaction of completing something in a single day. Why should it be any different for children?

The writing menu creates enthusiasm through choice and variety. Every child learns and brings knowledge back to the class, but it is presented in songs, posters, shadowboxes, lists, reports, interviews, and other formats. Since the projects are written during several weeks, kids have some leeway in completion times, writing at home, and choosing projects that appeal to them.

What differences in children should be considered?

Kids. In the newborn nursery they all look so similar. Hidden beneath those cooing, soft-skinned exteriors, however, lurk a myriad of differences that will show up in a few years. We must take into considerations such factors as:

* Brain dominance
* Preferred learning style
* Attention span
* Cultural background
* Birth order

* Learning disabilities
* Physical development
* Intelligence quotient
* Personal experiences
* Family relationships

If teachers want to be successful in teaching kids to write, we have to take some of these differences into consideration when we plan our writing strategies and assignments. What might be a joy to one child could be a death sentence to another. What one kid might accomplish in two days could take another child a week or more.

I remember when my fourth grade class was assigned to write and present original speeches on famous Americans. I have a black belt in talking. I could hardly wait for speech day. Other kids, though, broke out in hives and came down with strange symptoms. They prayed for communicable diseases so they wouldn't have to come to school on the appointed day. No wonder so many people hate writing: their own particular style, voice, and method of expression has never been unlocked. Freedom and choice are keys to success.

How do kids contribute knowledge to the class using the writing menu?

Think about the number of days you were in elementary school. How many do you actually remember? Most of the days we recall included personal involvement: participating in a play, an art contest, a kickball game, a science experiment.

Let's imagine that your class will be studying a new unit on Black History. Your goal is for your students to learn as much information as possible during the next four weeks about contributions made by Black Americans. You could teach all the information and assign reports. Instead, you present a writing menu with a number of activities about Black Americans that vary in style, genre, difficulty, and creativity. Some might take several days to complete. Others are short.

Students choose projects that appeal to their interests, learning styles, and abilities. All during the four weeks, students research, write, revise, and present knowledge they have gained through any number of writing activities. For example, the class learns about the life of Dr. Martin Luther King, Jr. through short plays, speeches, mock interviews, lists of contributions, and photo essays. Students actively participate in the learning process and embrace knowledge. At the same time they learn to express vital information to their peers. Kids become:

Writers
Researchers
Time Managers
Decision Makers
Employees
Self-Disciplinarians
Presenters
Appreciators
Teachers
Assessors

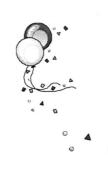

What age groups can use the writing menu?

With a little alteration, the writing menu system can be used successfully by K-12, elementary, middle school, or high school. Children as young as kindergarten benefit from choice and variety. The older students get, the more appealing the writing menu becomes. The success of the writing menu is not limited by age.

CHAPTER TWO
Getting Started: Planning Writing Menus

Start slowly.

You can implement writing menus on your own, but to start with, it works well to enlist the help of your fellow grade-level teachers or those on your teaching team. Agree to give the writing menu a short-run trial for a week or two. Using current teaching themes and topics as guides, come up with a simple writing menu with limited choices, perhaps three or four. I like a system where every teacher has input; it allows those creative juices to flow. Try writing menus for the trial period and then regroup to discuss successes, suggestions, etc.

What is the best way to plan a writing menu?

Writing needs to be purposeful. The more you tie factual knowledge, creativity, and self-expression to meaningful writing, the more kids will be able to relate to it. Use current topics of study from the disciplines you teach: science, reading, history, math, English, or social studies. First of all, list things your class will study during the next few weeks:

- ✓ Tall Tales
- ✓ Addition Facts
- ✓ Native Americans
- ✓ Community Helpers
- ✓ The Tropical Rain Forest

Now divide your writing menu into three categories such as:

Appetizers (or Snacks) - Easy projects such as listing, labeling, or naming that can be completed within a few minutes or one class session

Main Courses (or Full Meals) - Projects that involve multiple skills and take several days or weeks to complete

Desserts - Projects that involve kinesthetic expression, art, music, photography, dance, movement, and take several days to complete

Create writing assignments that go with each category of the writing menu. Keep in mind different learning styles, attention spans, and individual needs and interests. You will also want to consider specific grade-appropriate target skills as outlined in Chapter Three.

Here are some examples of appetizers you might use for older elementary or middle school students. Each of these projects involves simple skills and shorter time spans to complete. Appetizers are beneficial for children with lower skills, novice writers, or ESOL. They are also good choices when students are waiting for help from the teacher or when they need a break from a longer project.

Appetizers

1. List animals that can be found in a tropical rain forest.
   5 animals = 1 point possible

2. Write a complete sentence that includes a scientific fact about a rain forest animal. = 3 points possible

3. Write a sentence about a specific way we use addition to help us at home. Be sure to use who, what, when, where, why, and how. Each sentence = 3 points possible

4. Make a list of community helpers right here in our own town. Each helper = 1 point possible

5. Label items on the drawing of the Native American village. 1 item = 1 point possible

6. Cut out a picture of a community helper and glue it to a sheet of paper. Name 5 ways this person helps our community. 5 ways = 8 points possible

As you can see, each selection is simple and represents a short time span of completion. You will also notice there is a point value for each selection. Points are optional, but I recommend them for two reasons: they help kids make value judgements and they are great incentives to use time wisely.

Chapter Five will describe the point system in detail.

While appetizers just whet the writing appetite, main courses are "meatier." Main courses are writing projects that take planning, require brainstorming, and need a longer period of time for completion. Naturally, they will be worth more points. Main courses can be worked on for several weeks, interspersed with other selections from the writing menu.

I encourage students to work first on the writing portion of the main course in class so I can help them with that phase. I make sure I am available to trouble-shoot or to help with revision and suggestions. Home is a good place for kids to work on rewrites, artwork, costumes, props, etc., although they are free to do some of that during writing workshop as long as their writing portion is complete. Here are some examples of main courses:

Main Courses

1. We have read some really neat tall tales lately. Write your own tall tale about something that is outrageous or exaggerated. Remember that tall tales are usually funny and teach us some kind of lesson or truth. Ask 5 students to read your rough draft and make suggestions that will improve your story. Revise several times and write a final draft or type it on the computer. You may add your own artwork or pictures to illustrate your story.
25 points possible

2. Pretend you are a Native American living in an Indian Village 200 years ago. Write a diary about one week of your life and tell the exciting and adventurous things you do each day. Make sure you include how you find food, who teaches you special skills, and details of Native American life. Make your diary look like it was really written by someone who lived a long time ago.
25 points possible

3. Interview a real community helper. Write your questions in advance so you'll cover who, what, when, where, why, and how. Tape the interview or take careful notes. Write a report describing the helper's job, his training, and why we need this person in our community. Take a photo to go along with your report or draw the person's picture. 25 points possible

4. Pretend you are a research scientist in the rain forest of Panama. Write a letter inviting a class of school children to spend a week with you in the jungle. Tell them what they will see, what they will do each day, where they will stay, and what they should bring. 20 points possible

5. Plan an imaginary field trip for our class to a tropical rain forest. Tell us the number of miles we will have to travel, what kind of transportation we will need, the cost for the trip, what supplies we will need to bring, how long we will be gone, and our final destination. You may use a calculator, the catalogues on the book table, an atlas, maps, books, pamphlets, or the Internet to help you find information. You may write your field trip as a travel brochure with pictures, as a report, or give it as a speech using props. 25 points possible

6. Write a report about a famous Native American. Give some of his biographical information and write about the accomplishments of his life. Explain why this person is important in American history. Use several sources of research and put the information in your own words. Include pictures or maps that will make your report more interesting. 25 points possible

According to the needs of your class, you might decide to require each student to complete at least one main course. They may choose an appetizer or two and a dessert, if they wish, but a main course is a requirement. Other teachers will prefer to let kids choose whatever they want to write during the time you will use a writing menu and work towards accruing points. Either way can be successful.

Most of the time students will write and work on projects during the writing workshop. However, writing menus generate a lot of enthusiasm, and kids will want to work on them when they have free time or at home. It is not unusual for kids to ask if they can write extra projects at home since class time is limited. This is a good way for parents to see what kids are writing about and are learning in class.

**66 Changing a writer's focus
for a day or two can stimulate creativity. 99**

Desserts will appeal to those kids who like to share their creative talents or try something a little out of the ordinary. They are playful, light, and fun. Who says you can't eat dessert first?

Desserts

1. Write a commercial about a new television math game show for kids. Name the show and tell a little about the game, the rules, what kids will have to know, and the challenges. You may tape your commercial with the video camera or do it "live," in front of the class. Make it fun and exciting, but be sure you include who, what, when, where, why, and how.   15 points possible

2. Write a limerick about an animal that lives in the tropical rain forest. Teach us an interesting fact!   10 points possible

3. Write a letter to one of our community helpers. Thank her for the job she does and tell her why she is important to our town. 10 points possible

4. Write a message in a bottle written by a scientist in the rain forest who is trapped on the Amazon and needs help. Tell what happened, how he can be reached, and what help he needs. Put the message in a real bottle and tell the class a pretend story of who found the message and how the scientist was helped. 15 points possible

5. Write a menu for Paul Bunyan, his fellow lumberjacks, and his blue ox, Babe. Remember, these guys have HUGE appetites. Describe foods, amounts they might eat, and how these dishes would be prepared. Make us laugh! 15 points possible

6. Write a Native American song for the harvest season. Use the songs in our social studies book as an example. Include lyrics that teach us something about Indian agriculture. Make an instrument at home to accompany yourself. You may present your song on video tape or "live," before the class. 15 points possible

Grade-Level Writing Overview

Kindergarten
K

Verbalization, Drawing, Sounds, Letters, Words, Sentences, Sequencing, Oral Writing Games

First Grade
1

Verbalization, Drawing, Sounds, Letters, Words, Sequencing, Multiple Sentences, Oral Writing Games

Second Grade
2

The Basic Paragraph, Reports, Genres, Simple Narratives, Oral Writing Games

Third Grade
3

Multiple-Paragraph Essays, Reports, Genres, Complex Narratives, Oral Writing Games

Fourth Grade
4

Five-Paragraph Essays, Reports, Genres, Complex Narratives, Oral Writing Games

Fifth Grade
5

Five-Paragraph Essays, Reports, Genres, Complex Narratives, Cooperative Research

Sixth Grade
6

Five-Paragraph Essays, Reports, Genres, Complex Narratives, Independent Research

Seventh Grade
7

Five-Paragraph Essays, Reports, Genres, Complex Narratives, Research Papers, Comparisons, Persuasion, Educational Use of Internet

Eighth Grade
8

Five-Paragraph Essays, Reports, Genres, Complex Narratives, Research Papers, Comparisons, Persuasion, Debate, Educational Use of Internet

Writing Menu Pre-Planning

Month of _____

Grade_____   Quarter _____ Year _____

Teachers

_____

_____

Classroom Units, Themes, Topics of Study for This Menu

_____

_____

_____

New Writing Target Skills to be Introduced

_____

_____

_____

Writing Target Skills to Review

_____

_____

_____

Writing Target Skills to be Tested

_____

_____

_____

Genres and Writing Projects for This Menu

_____

_____

_____

More Ideas for Writing Menu Selections...

Narrative Account
Creative Short Story
Fictionalized Interview
Live Interview
Phone Interview
Puppet Play
Choral Reading
Classroom Play
Video Drama
"Soap Opera" Series
Quiz Questions
Newspaper Article
Original Poetry
Limerick
Picture Book
Movie Script
Letter to a Celebrity
Fictionalized Diary
Time-Travel Description
Personal Journal
Advice Column
Chapter Book
Job Description
Cartoons/Comic Strip
Helium-Balloon Message
Phone Message
Invitation to an Event
Message in a Bottle

Letter of Appreciation
Pen-Pal Letter
Secret Code
Song Lyrics
Thank-You Letter
Letter of Complaint
Treasure Map and Directions
Fictional Town Map
Photography and Captions
Shadow Box
Monologue
Original Speech
"Guess Who?" Biography
Autobiographical Story
Labels for Cans or Food Products
Magnifying-Glass Description
Radio Drama
Hobby Description
Slide Presentation/Voice Over
Book Review
Movie Review
Restaurant Review
Editorial for City Newspaper
Current-Events Synopsis
Daily or Weekly Weather Report
Commercial for a Product
Advertisement Layout
Certificate of Accomplishment

How many selections should a writing menu have?

That depends.

The number of writing menu selections will depend on the ages and abilities of your students. As mentioned in the beginning of this chapter, start slowly. While you are still in the initial stages of introducing the writing menu to your students, limit their choices to just a few items. Three to four selections might be appropriate for fourth or fifth grades, whereas two to three might be more feasible for second and third grades. Gradually, as your students catch on, add more choices to subsequent writing menus.

A list of menu ideas is provided for you on Page 12. In addition to appetizers, main courses, and desserts, you might decide to have one blank space entitled:

Another Great Idea _____

Some kids like to come up with creative ideas of their own, and as long as these are approved in advance by the teacher, they can be a healthy addition to any writing menu. Besides, you might get a new slant on what types of topics, projects, and genres individual children find interesting.

Examples of simplified writing menu selections for younger kids, emergent writers, or students with limitations are detailed for you in Chapter Ten.

How long should selections take to complete?

Main courses are multi-faceted and require at least several days to a week to complete. Appetizers are simpler and can be accomplished in a single writing workshop session. Desserts are more "fun" but sometimes require several days.

This variety allows children to vary their activities from day to day and fill short amounts of time, if needed. Writer's block, late arrival, a short attention span, or the need for a teacher's help don't have to prevent a child from making good use of his time. He can select a shorter project from the lists of appetizers or desserts until he is able to return to his main course project.

Variation in the life of an author is a good thing. Sometimes kids are eager to write volumes, other days they can hardly stand to look at a sheet of paper. Some days they are motivated to make progress on a longer project, and other days they'd have a more positive experience by successfully completing a short assignment. Changing a writer's focus for a day or two can stimulate creativity.

Writing Menu PlanningTips

- ✓ Plan menus to go with units, themes, topics of study.
- ✓ Consult grade-appropriate writing target skills.
- ✓ Target skills you've taught and modeled often.
- ✓ Take into consideration each child's interests.
- ✓ Take into consideration each child's abilities.
- ✓ Tap into multi-cultural and ethnic knowledge.
- ✓ Generate projects that highlight a variety of skill levels.
- ✓ Generate projects that require a variety of times to complete.
- ✓ Utilize multiple genres and formats.
- ✓ Create some projects that require drawing and artistic expression.
- ✓ Create some projects that highlight music, singing, acting or speech.
- ✓ Encourage high order, subjective, creative responses.
- ✓ Provide art supplies for children to use at home to enhance writing.
- ✓ Familiarize your students with the point value system.
- ✓ Encourage kids to teach new facts and knowledge to the class.

What learning styles should teachers consider?

The visual learner translates information into images or pictures in her brain. She responds well to written text and translates what she reads into a visual format by converting the words into mental pictures. She gravitates towards traditional types of writing such as reports, essays, stories, and poetry.

The kinesthetic learner learns best by touching, doing, or feeling. He has an intrinsic need to be involved in the creative process through acting, speaking, art, role-playing, constructing, or hands-on projects.

The auditory learner grasps information by listening and repeating. Writing becomes easier for him if given a chance to "talk out" his plot, opinions, or viewpoint with a peer before starting to write. His strong points will be speeches, debates, storytelling, and explaining.

Other multiple intelligence theories include seven specific intelligences: **visual/spatial, verbal/linguistic, musical/rhythmic, logical/mathematical, bodily/kinesthetic, interpersonal,** and **intrapersonal.** It is essential to consider each child's unique way of learning when planning writing menus.

CHAPTER THREE
Target Skills: Building Success One Step at a Time

Creative self-expression is a lovely experience that comprises a unique part of human interaction. It is also a vital skill that serves us throughout our lifetimes. There are those who would criticize putting any guidelines on writing at all, fearing we might eliminate individuality, spontaneity, and natural expression.

I am very much in favor of allowing children to explore, experiment and express themselves through all manner of speech, drama, illustration, storytelling, and sharing of opinions, observations, and factual information.

However, writing combines and balances characteristics of both art and an academic discipline. We can't leave its mastery to chance. Just as a budding, young violinist has a course of study laid out for him, so fledgling writers need a course of study that guides them, step by step, towards mastery and proficiency.

Because of the variety of skills associated with writing, it helps to have some basic guidelines to facilitate teaching. The grade-appropriate target skills listed in this chapter were compiled as a mere starting point. Public, private, and home-school teachers who implement these writing target skills lists are hereby encouraged to tailor the lists to their individual schools and classrooms.

There are separate lists for kindergarten, first, second, third, fourth, fifth, sixth, and seventh and eighth grades. The lists have been broken down into five sections: writing, author skills, conventions, illustrations, and oral language. By following these general guidelines, teachers and students build common bodies of knowledge that expand from year to year. Teachers can support and add to the writing continuum by teaching specific skills targeted for mastery in a specific grade. Teachers, students, and parents can refer to a list of skills that are to be learned and used in student writing throughout the year.

❦ **Fledgling writers need a course of study that guides them, step by step, towards proficiency.** ❧

How do target skills encourage success?

Writing is built on a succession of individual skills. Targeting one specific skill at a time is a terrific way to build success for young writers. Let's face it. There are thousands of ways for children to "fail" at writing. However, by teaching one or two targeted skills at a time for kids to master and use, we put the emphasis on success. Just as a new bride won't produce a "perfect husband" by her constant criticism, a writing teacher won't produce free thinking, uninhibited writers by pointing out every flaw in her students' writing. However, almost every writer can achieve success if he has a single, targeted goal to focus on.

These isolated goals, or target skills, should be identified, taught, modeled, practiced, and mastered. Students can keep records of target skills they've used successfully. The resulting feeling of accomplishment encourages young writers to include these skills in their writing more often.

What is a good way to teach target skills?

One at a time.

Focus on one skill, teach it, demonstrate, model, show good examples, and allow your students to practice. When you think a specific skill has been mastered, test it, and check it off on the target skills chart. Encourage kids to use mastered skills in their writing and to keep their own chart of skills they have learned and used.

Be sure to do a thorough job of teaching the skill you expect kids to master. For example, if *dialogue* is the skill you desire, you would:

✓ 1. Talk about the importance of dialogue to character development and plot.
✓ 2. Show good examples of dialogue in a variety of stories, plays, etc.
✓ 3. Demonstrate how to create dialogue for specific characters.
    When you demonstrate, kids simply watch.
✓ 4. Give kids magazine pictures of several people and ask them to write a few lines of dialogue to go with the scene.
✓ 5. Model how to punctuate dialogue, make a dialogue punctuation chart, and post it in a prominent place in the room.
    When you model, students perform along with you.
✓ 6. Give practice assignments for students to work on at home.
✓ 7. Give a target skills test on dialogue.
✓ 8. Validate students who use dialogue in their writing.

"Class," you will eventually announce, "good dialogue will be our target skill for today's writing workshop. I'd like you to see if you can include some talking in the story you're working on. Remember that dialogue can tell us about the character's personality or give important plot clues."

Remind students that they can refer to the dialogue-punctuation chart posted in the room or examples of dialogue in books. As kids write or revise during the writing workshop, they "hit the target" by adding the skill you've asked for. Just by doing that one thing they can feel they have achieved success.

As kids revise rough drafts and add a specific target skill you've asked for, they are immediately validated by a feeling of accomplishment. For your part, try not to worry right now about similes, strong verbs, emotion words, spelling, or any other skill. The one thing you've asked for is dialogue. Later, as you guide your students through the revising process, you may choose to ask for a variety of target skills that add maturity, clarity, beauty, and creativity to writing.

To enhance your students' sense of achievement and just for the sheer fun of it, make a target skill display that looks like a huge archery target. Glue an inexpensive counter tap-bell like you might find near a cash register right over the bull's-eye. When students "hit the target" by using a particular target skill correctly, they get to ring the bell.

Why save students' writing?

Teachers often send writing papers home every week, unintentionally implying that writing is expendable, to be attempted and then abandoned. Nothing could be further from the truth. Ask students to keep lots of writing samples in their writers' notebooks for a longer period of time. These pieces are great sources for practicing target skills. As you teach new skills, kids can try them out in pieces of writing they've already written instead of having to write a new piece first and then use the target skill.

❝ A writing teacher won't produce free-thinking, uninhibited writers by pointing out every flaw in her students' writing. Validate progress and accomplishments. ❞

How do target skills fit in with the writing menu?

As you plan the writing menu, you and your fellow teachers will keep in mind certain specific target skills you want to emphasize for each upcoming day of the writing menu. At the beginning of each daily writing workshop you will review one or two skills and target those particular skills for that day.

In advance, you will let kids know what skills you are looking for that day. This way, as they work on their writing projects, they can try to incorporate those particular skills in their writing. As students become comfortable with "hitting the target," you can ask for several skills they're familiar with and one that's relatively new. Students practice using target skills by including them in daily writing.

After students have learned to master and use target skills, they can choose what skills they'd like to use in a piece of writing as well as the ones you've asked them to "hit." As students prepare their writing to be assessed at the end of a writing menu time period, they can record what target skills they've used in their pieces. This encourages progress and accountability and is a valuable tool for an assessment appointment with a student.

How should target skills be tested?

Testing target skills is an effective way to evaluate how much students have learned about the craft of writing. It's also helpful in compiling a writing grade and authentic assessment, and during conferences with students. Target skills tests are simple for teachers to give and practically painless for kids.

While students are out of the room, select a particular target skill you've taught, modeled, and practiced with your class many times. Coming up with a topic sentence is an example of one you might choose to test. Write a simple paragraph on the board but *leave off the topic sentence*. Instead, underline the space where the topic sentence could be.

Cover the paragraph with a map or pull-down screen of some sort. Cut strips of paper 2" x 11" and place one on each student's desk.

When your kids return, they'll immediately ask, "What's this for?" You smile and tell them they are going to take a test. After their prerequisite moans and griping, say, "But the test is *easy*. As a matter of fact, it's so *easy* that this little strip is your test paper. I've done all the *hard* work for you. All you have to do is write one little sentence." At this point they become interested. Taking a test on such a small piece of paper is a novelty.

You continue. "You kids have written such beautiful topic sentences lately I'm sure you've mastered that skill. I've written a simple paragraph. The only thing that's missing is the topic sentence. Please write a good topic sentence on this little slip of paper. That's all you have to do." Expose the paragraph and allow them to begin. Most students finish within a matter of five minutes or less.

The target skill test is simple to evaluate. You have previously taught that a *topic sentence has the main idea, but NO details*. (Chapter Nine) Kids either "get it," or they don't. Pass or fail. Or, you might establish a simple grading criteria and assign a letter grade. The tests are "graded" in a matter of a few minutes and returned to students.

Students who "hit the target" check off that skill on their target skills list. If there are a few students who failed to "hit the target," remediate them or ask one of your bright, shining stars to teach a mini-lesson on topic sentences later that afternoon or the next day. Allow students to practice and review good examples, then retest them later in the week.

You might want to test important target skills several times during the year to insure students still have a grasp on them. Encourage students to continue using target skills and writers tricks in all forms of expository and narrative writing.

Our job as writing teachers is to infuse knowledge, measure progress, and plan for success. Teaching and testing target skills is an effective, easy way to build knowledge, measure progress, and create feelings of accomplishment. These skills enhance every writing project of the writing menu.

Who should keep a record of mastered target skills?

Let students keep a record of the target skills they have mastered and used in their daily writing. They can check these skills off as they are tested and again later as they use target skills in their writing. This record of target skills can be used in assessment appointments between teachers and students, to refer to during writing workshop, or for kids to show parents their progress. Keep a target skills chart on each child for your own use for record keeping, monthly planning, and parent conferences.

Where can kids keep their lists of target skills as well as ongoing writing?

The best possible scenario is for children to have self-contained writers' notebooks. These notebooks are described in detail in *Dynamite Writing Ideas* (Melissa Forney, Maupin House Publishing, 1996). These one inch, plastic covered notebooks are divided into sections that keep kids' ongoing projects and target skills organized. Some key components of the writer's notebook are:

- ✓ **idea bank**
- ✓ **first line bank**
- ✓ **last line bank**
- ✓ **word bank**
- ✓ **name bank**
- ✓ **illustrations**

- ✓ **narrative writing**
- ✓ **expository writing**
- ✓ **publishing**
- ✓ **reference aids**
- ✓ **target skills charts**
- ✓ **plastic zip bag of writing supplies**

Writing Target Skills for Kindergarten

Student Name _____ **Year** _____

Writing

- ☐ write his name
- ☐ write letters of the alphabet
- ☐ write simple numbers
- ☐ write letters on a line
- ☐ write from left to right
- ☐ write from top to bottom
- ☐ write a simple list
- ☐ write a bank of familiar words (selected from Dolch words or reading words)
- ☐ write labels or captions for drawings
- ☐ write simple sentences
- ☐ write a simple expository piece (card, invitation, journal)

Conventions

- ☐ label drawing with correct initial consonants or related sounds
- ☐ separate words with a space
- ☐ use phonics to help spell and sound out words
- ☐ use uppercase and lowercase letters
- ☐ use end punctuation

Author Skills

- ☐ define a specific purpose for writing
- ☐ add more details to a story (revision)
- ☐ do simple word processing (beginning computer skills)
- ☐ keep an author's notebook
- ☐ sharpen pencil
- ☐ publish a piece of original work
- ☐ receive suggestions objectively
- ☐ receive compliments graciously

Illustration

- ☐ draw basic shapes
- ☐ draw recognizable nouns
- ☐ draw a static picture
- ☐ draw a picture to illustrate a story
- ☐ draw a picture that focuses on a specific topic
- ☐ draw a few sequences of a storyboard
- ☐ use color to enhance illustrations
- ☐ cut out magazine pictures to illustrate a story or concept

Oral Writing

- ☐ brainstorm ideas
- ☐ generate ideas for stories
- ☐ relate story to teacher for dictation
- ☐ retell a stock story in sequence
- ☐ tell an original story
- ☐ answer a question about his picture
- ☐ recall and repeat details of a story
- ☐ share from the author's chair
- ☐ describe things in a picture
- ☐ tell what happened
- ☐ describe basic action
- ☐ use basic color words
- ☐ use basic number words
- ☐ tell where something happened
- ☐ tell what someone said (dialogue)
- ☐ describe an emotion and its cause
- ☐ express an opinion
- ☐ give personal information
- ☐ make suggestions for other writers
- ☐ compliment another writer

Writing Target Skills for First Grade

Student Name _____ **Year**_____

Writing

- [ ] write his name
- [ ] write the date
- [ ] write letters of the alphabet
- [ ] write simple numbers
- [ ] write letters on a line
- [ ] write from left to right
- [ ] write from top to bottom
- [ ] copy from the board
- [ ] write a simple list
- [ ] write a bank of familiar words (selected from Dolch words, vocabulary, or reading words)
- [ ] write labels or captions for drawings
- [ ] write complete sentences
- [ ] write original stories with beginning, middle, and ending
- [ ] compose rough drafts
- [ ] write a simple expository piece (card, invitation, journal)
- [ ] write beginning transitions
- [ ] describe with adjectives
- [ ] write to address a practice prompt or story starter

Conventions

- [ ] label drawing with words
- [ ] separate all words with spaces
- [ ] use phonics to help spell and sound out words
- [ ] use inventive or temporary spelling
- [ ] spell some words correctly
- [ ] use uppercase and lowercase letters
- [ ] use punctuation marks
- [ ] capitalize first word in sentence

Author Skills

- [ ] define a specific purpose for writing
- [ ] know the meaning and purpose of expository writing
- [ ] know the meaning and purpose of narrative writing
- [ ] select topics of interest
- [ ] generate topics of interest
- [ ] use some form of pre-writing such as listing, webbing, or storyboard
- [ ] focus on a specific topic
- [ ] support an opinion or findings with details and reasons
- [ ] edit writing and find missing words or details
- [ ] work on a piece of writing through the course of several days
- [ ] add more details to a piece in draft form (revision)
- [ ] change some details of a piece in draft form (revision)
- [ ] copy a final draft in neat handwriting
- [ ] help formulate and use a rubric
- [ ] publish a piece of original work
- [ ] do simple word processing (beginning computer skills)
- [ ] keep an author's notebook
- [ ] keep writing supplies in order
- [ ] sharpen pencil
- [ ] receive suggestions objectively
- [ ] receive compliments graciously
- [ ] stay on task during writing workshop
- [ ] work somewhat independently
- [ ] find an alternate source of help when the teacher is occupied

...First Grade

Illustration

- [ ] draw basic shapes
- [ ] draw recognizable nouns
- [ ] draw pictures to illustrate a story
- [ ] draw pictures that focus on a given or specific topic
- [ ] draw 4 to 6 sequences of a storyboard (beginning, middle, end)
- [ ] use color to enhance illustrations
- [ ] work in multiple mediums to enhance illustration
- [ ] cut out magazine pictures to illustrate stories or concepts

66 **Teaching and testing target skills is an effective way to build knowledge, measure progress, and create feelings of accomplishment. These skills can enhance every writing project of the writing menu.** 99

Oral Writing

- [ ] brainstorm ideas
- [ ] generate ideas for stories (narrative)
- [ ] ask and answer questions
- [ ] paraphrase a story in his own words
- [ ] tell an original story
- [ ] create alternative endings to stories
- [ ] recall and repeat details of a story
- [ ] share from the author's chair
- [ ] describe things in a picture
- [ ] tell what happened
- [ ] describe basic action
- [ ] use basic color words
- [ ] use basic number words
- [ ] tell where something happened
- [ ] tell what someone said (dialogue)
- [ ] describe an emotion and its cause
- [ ] relate an interesting event and hold the attention of the group
- [ ] present a speech or oral report on an assigned topic
- [ ] express an opinion
- [ ] give personal information
- [ ] get to the point right away
- [ ] make suggestions for other writers
- [ ] conference with peer author
- [ ] create and communicate messages
- [ ] act out dramatizations of stories

Writing Target Skills for Second Grade

Student Name _____ **Year**_____

Writing

- [ ] write name and date on her work
- [ ] write detailed lists
- [ ] write complete sentences
- [ ] write a basic expository paragraph
- [ ] write original stories with beginning, middle, and ending
- [ ] compose rough drafts
- [ ] use transition words
- [ ] describe with adjectives
- [ ] use strong verbs
- [ ] describe with adverbs
- [ ] write to address a practice prompt or story starter
- [ ] record entries in a journal
- [ ] compare two things
- [ ] use specific emotion words
- [ ] use specific sensory words
- [ ] use juicy color words
- [ ] title her writing piece
- [ ] combine simple sentences to make one dense, mature sentence
- [ ] support her writing with facts, information, reasons
- [ ] vary sentence beginnings
- [ ] use spelling words and vocabulary words in her writing
- [ ] use a hook or grabber to capture the reader's attention

Conventions

- [ ] indent new paragraph
- [ ] separate all words with spaces
- [ ] use phonics to help spell and sound out words
- [ ] spell common words correctly
- [ ] use inventive or temporary spelling
- [ ] use mature, difficult words and attempt to spell them
- [ ] recognize some misspelled words
- [ ] use a dictionary to look up some words
- [ ] proofread and correct a rough draft
- [ ] use uppercase and lowercase letters
- [ ] use punctuation marks
- [ ] capitalize first word in sentence
- [ ] write legibly

Author Skills

- [ ] define a specific purpose for writing
- [ ] know the meaning and purpose of expository writing
- [ ] know the meaning and purpose of narrative writing
- [ ] select topics of interest
- [ ] generate topics of interest
- [ ] use some form of pre-writing such as listing, webbing, or storyboard
- [ ] focus on a specific topic
- [ ] support an opinion or findings with details and reasons
- [ ] edit writing and find missing words or details
- [ ] work on a piece of writing for several days

...Second Grade

...Author Skills

- [ ] add more details to a piece in draft form (revision)
- [ ] change some details of a piece in draft form (revision)
- [ ] copy a final draft in neat handwriting
- [ ] publish a piece of original work
- [ ] help formulate and use a rubric
- [ ] respond personally to literature
- [ ] do simple word processing (beginning computer skills)
- [ ] keep an author's notebook
- [ ] keep writing supplies in order
- [ ] have pencils sharpened and ready
- [ ] receive suggestions objectively
- [ ] receive compliments graciously
- [ ] stay on task during writing workshop
- [ ] work somewhat independently
- [ ] help a peer solve a writing problem
- [ ] find an alternate source of help when the teacher is occupied

Illustration

- [ ] draw basic shapes
- [ ] draw recognizable objects
- [ ] draw pictures to illustrate a story
- [ ] draw pictures that focus on a given or specific topic
- [ ] draw 6 to 8 sequences of a storyboard (beginning, middle, end)
- [ ] use color to enhance illustrations
- [ ] cut out magazine pictures to illustrate stories or concepts
- [ ] work in multiple mediums to enhance illustration

Oral Writing

- [ ] brainstorm ideas
- [ ] generate ideas for stories (narrative)
- [ ] ask and answer questions
- [ ] paraphrase a story in her own words
- [ ] tell an original story
- [ ] create alternative endings to stories
- [ ] recall and repeat details of a story
- [ ] share from the author's chair
- [ ] describe things in a picture
- [ ] tell what happened
- [ ] describe basic action
- [ ] use basic color words
- [ ] use basic number words
- [ ] tell where something happened
- [ ] tell what someone said (dialogue)
- [ ] describe an emotion and its cause
- [ ] relate an interesting event and hold the attention of the group
- [ ] present a speech or oral report on an assigned topic
- [ ] express an opinion
- [ ] give personal information
- [ ] get to the point right away
- [ ] make suggestions for other writers
- [ ] conference with peer author
- [ ] create and communicate messages
- [ ] act out dramatizations of stories

Writing Target Skills for Third Grade

Student Name _____ **Year**_____

Writing

- [ ] write name and date on work
- [ ] write detailed lists
- [ ] write complete sentences
- [ ] write a basic expository paragraph
- [ ] write several related paragraphs
- [ ] write original stories with beginning, middle, and ending
- [ ] include setting and time frame
- [ ] write a takeaway ending (what the main character learned or felt)
- [ ] write several genres (poetry, fairy tales, tall tales, chapter books)
- [ ] compose rough drafts
- [ ] use transition words
- [ ] describe with adjectives
- [ ] use strong verbs
- [ ] describe with adverbs
- [ ] write to address a practice prompt or story starter
- [ ] record entries in a journal
- [ ] compare two things
- [ ] use specific emotion words
- [ ] use specific sensory words
- [ ] use juicy color words
- [ ] use similes
- [ ] use dialogue with tags
- [ ] write an appropriate title
- [ ] take notes
- [ ] combine simple sentences to make one dense, mature sentence
- [ ] support writing with facts, information, reasons
- [ ] vary sentence beginnings
- [ ] use spelling words and vocabulary words in original writing
- [ ] use a hook or grabber to capture the reader's attention
- [ ] start the five-paragraph essay (second semester)

Conventions

- [ ] label drawing with captions
- [ ] space writing appropriately
- [ ] use phonics to help spell and sound out words
- [ ] spell common words correctly
- [ ] use inventive or temporary spelling
- [ ] use mature, difficult words and attempt to spell them
- [ ] recognize some misspelled words
- [ ] use a dictionary to look up words
- [ ] proofread and correct rough draft
- [ ] use uppercase and lowercase letters
- [ ] use punctuation marks
- [ ] indent
- [ ] capitalize first word in sentence
- [ ] write legibly

Author Skills

- [ ] define a specific purpose for writing
- [ ] know the meaning and purpose of expository writing
- [ ] know the meaning and purpose of narrative writing
- [ ] select topics of interest
- [ ] generate topics of interest
- [ ] narrow down a topic
- [ ] use some form of pre-writing such as listing, webbing, or storyboard
- [ ] focus on a specific topic
- [ ] support his opinion or findings with details and reasons
- [ ] identify the problem/solution before writing (narrative)
- [ ] identify the main emotion he wants the reader to feel
- [ ] work on a piece of writing for several days
- [ ] edit work and find missing words or details

...Third Grade

...Author Skills

- [ ] use a few basic proofreaders' marks
- [ ] add more details to a piece in draft form (revision)
- [ ] change some details of a piece in draft form (revision)
- [ ] substitute a more elaborate or precise word to clarify meaning
- [ ] copy a final draft in neat handwriting
- [ ] publish a piece of original work
- [ ] help formulate and use a rubric
- [ ] respond personally to literature
- [ ] gather research from several sources
- [ ] do simple word processing (beginning computer skills)
- [ ] keep an author's notebook
- [ ] keep writing supplies in order
- [ ] have pencils sharpened and ready
- [ ] receive suggestions objectively
- [ ] receive compliments graciously
- [ ] stay on task during writing workshop
- [ ] work independently
- [ ] help a peer solve a writing problem
- [ ] find an alternate source of help when the teacher is occupied

Illustration

- [ ] draw familiar objects and people
- [ ] draw pictures to illustrate a story
- [ ] draw pictures that demonstrate action
- [ ] draw pictures that focus on a given or specific topic
- [ ] draw 8 to 10 sequences of a storyboard (beginning, middle, end)
- [ ] demonstrate creativity and originality
- [ ] use imagination and fantasy
- [ ] use color to enhance illustrations
- [ ] cut out magazine pictures to illustrate stories or concepts
- [ ] work in multiple mediums to enhance illustration

Oral Writing

- [ ] brainstorm ideas
- [ ] generate ideas for stories
- [ ] ask and answer questions
- [ ] paraphrase a story in his own words
- [ ] tell an original story
- [ ] create alternative endings to stories
- [ ] recall and repeat details of a story
- [ ] share from the author's chair
- [ ] describe things in a picture
- [ ] create imagined scenarios from magazine pictures or photos
- [ ] use juicy color words
- [ ] use quantitative words
- [ ] tell setting and time frame
- [ ] tell what someone said (dialogue)
- [ ] describe an emotion, its cause, and tell why he can relate to it
- [ ] relate an interesting event and hold the attention of the group
- [ ] present a speech or oral report on an assigned topic
- [ ] use facial expression and vocal inflection when telling a story
- [ ] express an opinion
- [ ] defend his opinion with supporting details and reasons
- [ ] get to the point right away
- [ ] make suggestions for other writers
- [ ] conference with peer authors
- [ ] create and communicate messages
- [ ] act out dramatizations of stories

Writing Target Skills for Fourth Grade

Student Name _____ **Year** _____

Writing

- [ ] write name and date on her work
- [ ] write detailed lists
- [ ] write complete sentences
- [ ] write a basic expository paragraph
- [ ] write multiple related paragraphs
- [ ] write original stories with beginning, middle, and ending
- [ ] include setting and time frame
- [ ] write a "takeaway ending" (what the main character learned)
- [ ] write several genres (poetry, fairy tales, tall tales, chapter stories)
- [ ] write several kinds of letters and address envelopes
- [ ] compose rough drafts
- [ ] use transitional phrases smoothly so thoughts flow in logical order
- [ ] describe with adjectives
- [ ] use strong verbs
- [ ] describe with adverbs
- [ ] write to address a practice prompt or story starter
- [ ] record entries in a journal
- [ ] contrast and compare
- [ ] use specific emotion words
- [ ] use specific sensory words
- [ ] use juicy color words
- [ ] use similes
- [ ] use metaphors
- [ ] use tagged and tagless dialogue and include quotation marks
- [ ] title her writing piece
- [ ] take notes and outline
- [ ] summarize
- [ ] combine simple sentences to make dense, mature sentences
- [ ] support her writing with facts, information, reasons
- [ ] vary sentence beginnings with clauses
- [ ] use spelling words and vocabulary words in original compositions

...Writing

- [ ] use a hook or grabber to capture the reader's attention
- [ ] write the five-paragraph essay

Conventions

- [ ] spell common words correctly
- [ ] use inventive or temporary spelling
- [ ] use a mature, difficult word, rather than a common word, and attempt to spell it
- [ ] recognize most misspelled words
- [ ] use a dictionary to look up words
- [ ] proofread and correct rough draft
- [ ] use punctuation marks and indent
- [ ] use quotation marks
- [ ] capitalize first word in sentence
- [ ] write legibly

Author Skills

- [ ] define a specific purpose for writing
- [ ] identify the audience before writing
- [ ] know the meaning and purpose of expository writing
- [ ] know the meaning and purpose of narrative writing
- [ ] distinguish the differences between narrative and expository prompts
- [ ] select topics of interest
- [ ] generate topics of interest
- [ ] narrow down a broad topic
- [ ] work on several projects in various stages of completion
- [ ] use some form of pre-writing such as listing, webbing, or storyboard
- [ ] focus on and maintain a main idea
- [ ] support opinion or findings with details and reasons
- [ ] identify the problem/solution before writing (narrative)
- [ ] identify the main emotion she wants the reader to feel

...Fourth Grade

...Author Skills

- [ ] work on a piece of writing for several days
- [ ] edit writing and find missing words or details
- [ ] use basic proofreaders' marks
- [ ] add more details to a piece in draft form (revision)
- [ ] change various details of a piece in draft form (revision)
- [ ] substitute a more elaborate or precise word to clarify meaning
- [ ] copy a final draft in neat handwriting
- [ ] publish a piece of original work
- [ ] help formulate and use a rubric
- [ ] respond personally to literature
- [ ] gather research from several sources
- [ ] use the computer as a writing tool
- [ ] keep an author's notebook
- [ ] keep writing supplies in order
- [ ] have pencils sharpened and ready
- [ ] receive and give suggestions
- [ ] receive and give compliments
- [ ] stay on task during writing workshop
- [ ] work independently and in groups
- [ ] help a peer solve a writing problem
- [ ] find an alternate source of help when the teacher is occupied

Illustration

- [ ] draw familiar objects and people
- [ ] draw pictures to illustrate a story
- [ ] draw pictures that demonstrate action
- [ ] draw pictures that focus on a given or specific topic
- [ ] draw 10 - 12 sequences of a storyboard (beginning, middle, end)
- [ ] draw maps and diagrams
- [ ] demonstrate creativity and originality
- [ ] use imagination and fantasy
- [ ] use color to enhance illustrations
- [ ] use original artwork, magazine pictures, photos, or music to illustrate stories or concepts

Oral Writing

- [ ] brainstorm ideas
- [ ] generate ideas for stories (narrative)
- [ ] ask and answer questions
- [ ] paraphrase a story in her own words
- [ ] tell an original story
- [ ] create alternative endings to stories
- [ ] recall and repeat details of a story
- [ ] share from the author's chair
- [ ] describe things in a picture
- [ ] create imagined scenarios from magazine pictures or photos
- [ ] tell setting and time frame
- [ ] show personality traits and story clues by using clever dialogue
- [ ] describe an emotion, its cause, and tell why she can relate to it
- [ ] relate an interesting event and hold the attention of the group
- [ ] present a speech or oral report on a specific topic
- [ ] use facial and vocal expression
- [ ] express an opinion without putting someone else down
- [ ] defend her opinion with supporting details and reasons
- [ ] get to the point right away
- [ ] make suggestions for other writers
- [ ] conference with peer authors
- [ ] create and communicate messages
- [ ] act out dramatizations of stories

Writing Target Skills for Fifth Grade

Student Name _____ **Year** _____

Writing

- ☐ write name and date on his work
- ☐ write detailed lists
- ☐ write complete sentences
- ☐ write a basic expository paragraph
- ☐ write multiple related paragraphs
- ☐ write original stories with beginning, middle, and ending
- ☐ write stories with multiple problems and solutions
- ☐ include setting and time frame
- ☐ write a "takeaway ending" (what the main character learned or felt)
- ☐ write multiple genres (poetry, fairy tales, tall tales, chapter stories)
- ☐ experiment with style and viewpoint
- ☐ use literary devices
- ☐ keep writing in one tense
- ☐ use active, rather than passive, verbs
- ☐ write many kinds of letters and address envelopes
- ☐ persuade the reader by using strong, emotional language
- ☐ compose rough drafts
- ☐ use transitional phrases smoothly so thoughts flow in logical order
- ☐ describe with adjectives
- ☐ use strong verbs
- ☐ describe with adverbs
- ☐ write to address a practice prompt or story starter
- ☐ record entries in a journal
- ☐ contrast and compare
- ☐ use specific emotion words
- ☐ use specific sensory words
- ☐ use juicy color words
- ☐ use similes
- ☐ use metaphors
- ☐ use onomatopoeia
- ☐ use tagged and tagless dialogue and include quotation marks
- ☐ write an appropriate title
- ☐ take notes and outline
- ☐ summarize

...Writing

- ☐ combine simple sentences to make dense, mature sentences
- ☐ support writing with facts, information, reasons
- ☐ vary sentence beginnings with clauses
- ☐ vary sentence length
- ☐ use spelling words and vocabulary words in original compositions
- ☐ use a hook or grabber to capture the reader's attention
- ☐ write five-paragraph essays

Conventions

- ☐ spell most words correctly
- ☐ use inventive or temporary spelling
- ☐ use a mature, difficult word, rather than a common word, and attempt to spell it
- ☐ recognize misspelled words
- ☐ use a dictionary to look up words
- ☐ use a thesaurus to enhance diction
- ☐ proofread and correct rough draft
- ☐ use punctuation marks and indent
- ☐ use quotation marks
- ☐ capitalize first word in sentence
- ☐ write legibly

Author Skills

- ☐ define a specific purpose for writing
- ☐ identify the audience before writing
- ☐ know the meaning and purpose of expository writing
- ☐ know the meaning and purpose of narrative writing
- ☐ distinguish the differences between narrative and expository prompts
- ☐ select topics of interest
- ☐ generate topics of interest
- ☐ narrow down a broad topic
- ☐ work on several projects in various stages of completion
- ☐ use some form of pre-writing such as listing, webbing, or storyboard

...Fifth Grade

...Author Skills

- ☐ focus on and maintain a main idea
- ☐ support opinion or findings with details and reasons
- ☐ identify the problem/solution before writing (narrative)
- ☐ identify the main emotion he wants the reader to feel
- ☐ work on a piece of writing for several days
- ☐ edit writing and find missing words or details
- ☐ use basic proofreaders' marks
- ☐ add more details to a piece in draft form (revision)
- ☐ change various details of a piece in draft form (revision)
- ☐ substitute a more elaborate or precise word to clarify meaning
- ☐ copy a final draft in neat handwriting
- ☐ publish a piece of original work
- ☐ help formulate and use a rubric
- ☐ respond personally to literature
- ☐ gather research from several sources
- ☐ use the computer as a writing tool
- ☐ keep an author's notebook
- ☐ keep writing supplies in order
- ☐ have pencils sharpened and ready
- ☐ receive and give suggestions
- ☐ receive and give compliments
- ☐ stay on task during writing workshop
- ☐ work independently and in groups
- ☐ help a peer solve a writing problem
- ☐ find an alternate source of help when the teacher is occupied

Illustration

- ☐ draw familiar objects and people
- ☐ draw pictures to illustrate a story
- ☐ draw pictures that demonstrate action
- ☐ draw pictures that focus on a topic
- ☐ draw 10 - 12 sequences of a storyboard (beginning, middle, end)
- ☐ draw maps and diagrams

...Illustration

- ☐ demonstrate creativity and originality
- ☐ use imagination and fantasy
- ☐ use color to enhance illustrations
- ☐ use original artwork, magazine pictures, photos, or music to illustrate stories or concepts

Oral Writing

- ☐ brainstorm ideas
- ☐ generate ideas for stories
- ☐ ask and answer questions
- ☐ paraphrase a story in his own words
- ☐ tell an original story
- ☐ create alternative endings to stories
- ☐ recall and repeat details of a story
- ☐ share from the author's chair
- ☐ describe things in a picture
- ☐ create imagined scenarios from magazine pictures or photos
- ☐ tell setting and time frame
- ☐ show personality traits and story clues by using clever dialogue
- ☐ describe an emotion, its cause, and tell why he can relate to it
- ☐ relate an interesting event and hold the attention of the group
- ☐ present a speech or oral report on a specific topic
- ☐ use facial and vocal expression
- ☐ express an opinion without putting someone else down
- ☐ defend his opinion with supporting details and reasons
- ☐ get to the point right away
- ☐ make suggestions for other writers
- ☐ conference with peer authors
- ☐ create and communicate messages
- ☐ act out dramatizations of stories

Writing Target Skills for Sixth Grade

Student Name _____ **Year**_____

Writing

- [ ] write name and date on her work
- [ ] write detailed lists
- [ ] write complete sentences
- [ ] write a basic expository paragraph
- [ ] write multiple related paragraphs
- [ ] write original stories, complex plots, and multiple characters
- [ ] write stories with multiple problems and solutions
- [ ] create setting and time frame
- [ ] write a "takeaway ending" (what the main character learned or felt)
- [ ] write multiple genres (poetry, fairy tales, tall tales, chapter stories)
- [ ] experiment with style and viewpoint
- [ ] use literary devices
- [ ] keep writing in one tense
- [ ] use active, rather than passive, verbs
- [ ] write many kinds of letters and address envelopes
- [ ] persuade the reader by using strong, emotional language
- [ ] compose rough drafts
- [ ] use transitional phrases smoothly so thoughts flow in logical order
- [ ] describe with adjectives
- [ ] use strong verbs
- [ ] describe with adverbs
- [ ] write to address a practice prompt or story starter
- [ ] record entries in a journal
- [ ] write critiques and reviews
- [ ] use specific emotion words
- [ ] use specific sensory words
- [ ] use juicy color words
- [ ] use similes
- [ ] use metaphors
- [ ] use onomatopoeia
- [ ] use tagged and tagless dialogue and include quotation marks
- [ ] write an appropriate title
- [ ] research, take notes, outline
- [ ] summarize and paraphrase

...Writing

- [ ] combine simple sentences to make dense, mature sentences
- [ ] support writing with many facts, information, reasons
- [ ] use clauses to enhance sentences
- [ ] vary sentence beginnings and length
- [ ] use spelling words and vocabulary words in original compositions
- [ ] use a hook or grabber to capture the reader's attention
- [ ] write essays and research papers

Conventions

- [ ] spell most words correctly
- [ ] use inventive or temporary spelling
- [ ] use a mature, difficult word, rather than a common word, and attempt to spell it
- [ ] recognize misspelled words
- [ ] use a dictionary to look up words
- [ ] use a thesaurus to enhance diction
- [ ] proofread and correct rough draft
- [ ] use punctuation marks and indent
- [ ] use quotation marks
- [ ] capitalize first word in sentence
- [ ] write legibly and/or type

Author Skills

- [ ] define a specific purpose for writing
- [ ] identify the audience before writing
- [ ] know the meaning and purpose of expository writing
- [ ] know the meaning and purpose of narrative writing
- [ ] distinguish the differences between narrative and expository prompts
- [ ] select topics of interest
- [ ] generate topics of interest
- [ ] narrow down a broad topic
- [ ] work on several projects in various stages of completion
- [ ] use some form of pre-writing such as listing, webbing, or storyboard

...Sixth Grade

...Author Skills

- [ ] focus on and maintain a main idea
- [ ] support opinion or findings with details and reasons
- [ ] identify the problem/solution before writing (narrative)
- [ ] identify the main emotion she wants the reader to feel
- [ ] work on a piece of writing for several weeks
- [ ] edit writing and find missing words or details
- [ ] use proofreaders' marks
- [ ] add more details to a piece in draft form (revision)
- [ ] change various details of a piece in draft form (revision)
- [ ] substitute a more elaborate or precise word to clarify meaning
- [ ] copy a final draft or type
- [ ] publish pieces of original work
- [ ] use a rubric to improve writing
- [ ] respond personally to literature
- [ ] gather research from many sources
- [ ] use the computer as a writing tool
- [ ] keep an author's notebook
- [ ] keep writing supplies in order
- [ ] have pencils sharpened and ready
- [ ] receive and give suggestions
- [ ] receive and give compliments
- [ ] stay on task during writing workshop
- [ ] work independently and in groups
- [ ] help a peer solve a writing problem
- [ ] find an alternate source of help when the teacher is occupied

Illustration

- [ ] draw familiar objects and people
- [ ] draw pictures to illustrate a story
- [ ] draw pictures that demonstrate action
- [ ] draw pictures that focus on a topic
- [ ] draw 10 - 12 sequences of a storyboard (beginning, middle, end)
- [ ] draw maps and diagrams

...Illustration

- [ ] demonstrate creativity and originality
- [ ] use imagination and fantasy
- [ ] use color to enhance illustrations
- [ ] use original artwork, magazine pictures, photos, or music to illustrate stories or concepts

Oral Writing

- [ ] brainstorm ideas
- [ ] generate ideas for stories (narrative)
- [ ] ask and answer questions
- [ ] paraphrase a story in her own words
- [ ] tell an original story
- [ ] create alternative endings to stories
- [ ] recall and repeat details of a story
- [ ] share from the author's chair
- [ ] teach writing "mini-lessons"
- [ ] create imagined scenarios from magazine pictures or photos
- [ ] recreate a familiar story in a unique or different setting and time frame
- [ ] show personality traits and story clues by using clever dialogue
- [ ] describe an emotion, its cause, and tell why she can relate to it
- [ ] relate an interesting event and hold the attention of the group
- [ ] present a speech, oral report, or debate on a topic of high interest
- [ ] use facial and vocal expression
- [ ] express an opinion without putting someone else down
- [ ] defend his opinion with supporting details and reasons
- [ ] get to the point right away
- [ ] make suggestions for other writers
- [ ] conference with peer authors
- [ ] create and communicate messages
- [ ] act out dramatizations of stories

Target Skills for Seventh and Eighth Grade

Student Name _____ **Year**_____

Writing

- [ ] write name and date on his work
- [ ] write detailed lists
- [ ] write complete sentences
- [ ] write a basic expository paragraph
- [ ] write multiple related paragraphs
- [ ] write original stories, complex plots and multiple characters
- [ ] write stories with multiple problems and solutions
- [ ] create setting and time frame
- [ ] write a "takeaway ending"
- [ ] write multiple genres (poetry, fairy tales, tall tales, chapter stories)
- [ ] experiment with style and viewpoint
- [ ] use literary devices
- [ ] keep writing in one tense
- [ ] use active rather than passive verbs
- [ ] write many kinds of letters and address envelopes
- [ ] persuade the reader by using strong, emotional language
- [ ] keep a diary or journal
- [ ] use transitional phrases smoothly so thoughts flow in logical order
- [ ] describe with adjectives
- [ ] use strong verbs
- [ ] describe with adverbs
- [ ] write to address a practice prompt or story starter
- [ ] record entries in a journal
- [ ] write critiques and reviews
- [ ] use specific emotion words
- [ ] use specific sensory words
- [ ] use juicy color words
- [ ] use similes and metaphors
- [ ] use onomatopoeia
- [ ] use tagged and tagless dialogue and include quotation marks
- [ ] write an appropriate title
- [ ] research, take notes, outline
- [ ] summarize and paraphrase
- [ ] use the Internet for research
- [ ] analyze a piece of literature

...Writing

- [ ] combine simple sentences to make dense, mature sentences
- [ ] support writing with many facts, information, reasons
- [ ] use clauses to enhance sentences
- [ ] vary sentence beginnings and length
- [ ] write an original play
- [ ] use a hook or grabber to capture the reader's attention
- [ ] write essays and research papers

Conventions

- [ ] spell most words correctly
- [ ] use inventive or temporary spelling
- [ ] use a mature, difficult word, rather than a common word, and attempt to spell it
- [ ] recognize misspelled words
- [ ] use a dictionary to look up words
- [ ] use a thesaurus to enhance diction
- [ ] proofread and correct rough draft
- [ ] use punctuation marks and indent
- [ ] use quotation marks correctly
- [ ] capitalize first word in sentence
- [ ] write legibly and/or type

Author Skills

- [ ] define a specific purpose for writing
- [ ] identify the audience before writing
- [ ] know the meaning and purpose of expository writing
- [ ] know the meaning and purpose of narrative writing
- [ ] distinguish the differences between narrative and expository prompts
- [ ] select topics of interest
- [ ] generate topics of interest
- [ ] narrow a broad topic
- [ ] work on several projects in various stages of completion
- [ ] use some form of pre-writing such as listing, webbing, or storyboard

...Seventh and Eighth Grade

...Author Skills

- [ ] focus on and maintain a main idea
- [ ] support opinion or findings with details and reasons
- [ ] identify the problem/solution before writing (narrative)
- [ ] identify the main emotion he wants the reader to feel
- [ ] work on a piece of writing throughout several weeks
- [ ] edit writing and find missing words or details
- [ ] use proofreaders' marks
- [ ] add more details to a piece in draft form (revision)
- [ ] change various details of a piece in draft form (revision)
- [ ] substitute a more elaborate or precise word to clarify meaning
- [ ] copy a final draft or type
- [ ] publish pieces of original work
- [ ] use a rubric to improve writing
- [ ] respond personally to literature
- [ ] gather research from many sources
- [ ] use the computer as a writing tool
- [ ] keep an author's notebook
- [ ] keep writing supplies in order
- [ ] have pencils sharpened and ready
- [ ] receive and give suggestions
- [ ] receive and give compliments
- [ ] stay on task during writing workshop
- [ ] work independently and in groups
- [ ] help a peer solve a writing problem
- [ ] find an alternate source of help when the teacher is occupied

Illustration

- [ ] draw familiar objects and people
- [ ] draw pictures to illustrate a story
- [ ] draw pictures that demonstrate action
- [ ] draw pictures that focus on a topic
- [ ] draw 10 - 12 sequences of a storyboard (beginning, middle, end)
- [ ] draw maps and diagrams

...Illustration

- [ ] demonstrate creativity and originality
- [ ] use imagination and fantasy
- [ ] use color to enhance illustrations
- [ ] use original artwork, magazine pictures, photos, or music to illustrate stories or concepts

Oral Writing

- [ ] brainstorm ideas
- [ ] generate ideas for stories (narrative)
- [ ] ask and answer questions
- [ ] paraphrase a story in his own words
- [ ] tell an original story
- [ ] create alternative endings to stories
- [ ] recall and repeat details of a story
- [ ] memorize and quote poetry
- [ ] teach writing "mini-lessons"
- [ ] make comparisons
- [ ] recreate a familiar story in a unique or different setting and time frame
- [ ] show personality traits and story clues by using clever dialogue
- [ ] identify and express his values
- [ ] relate an interesting event and hold the attention of the group
- [ ] present a speech, oral report, or debate on a topic of high interest
- [ ] use facial and vocal expression
- [ ] express an opinion without putting someone else down
- [ ] defend his opinion with supporting details and reasons
- [ ] get to the point right away
- [ ] conduct a personal interview
- [ ] hold a conference with peer authors
- [ ] create and communicate messages
- [ ] act out dramatizations of stories
- [ ] negotiate through differences of opinion with teacher and peers

CHAPTER FOUR

On Your Mark, Get Set, GO: Introducing Writing Menus

Kids love adventure. Teachers are usually scared to death to try something new.

Explain to your class that you are going to let them try a different system you think they'll really like: choosing writing assignments from a menu, budgeting their own time, making their own decisions. The kicker is they have to stay on task and produce a body of work. Earning points is an added bonus. Those kids who aren't able to make wise choices will have more structured assignments until they can prove themselves.

Distribute copies of the new writing menu. Let kids study it for a while and discuss it with other students, then have a class discussion. Review the menu together. Answer questions. Don't squelch excitement. Keep things positive.

If you decide to use a point system, give out copies of a simple, clear-cut point sheet. Review the point sheet thoroughly. Explain what benefits will be rewarded for accrued points, how to earn extra points, and what will cause points to be taken off a writing project. You might choose to use the Bonus Points Bucks on page 45 as a reward for extra special behavior or projects.

Distribute copies of sample student contracts and discuss the importance of entering into an agreement. Send a copy of the point sheet, writing menu, and contract home to parents with a short letter of explanation. A prototype is on page 41. Let kids have several days to think about possible choices, to discuss these with their parents, and to consider their options. Build up the writing menu system as an exciting, new way to give purpose and meaning to learning and writing.

Kids need good examples. Let them examine collections of student work in many genres so they can formulate ideas of things they'd like to try. Ask which projects appeal to them and why. Encourage kids to analyze what types of projects would cause them to stretch their abilities. Explain how writing menus will prepare kids for real-life situations in their future jobs and careers.

66 We're not looking for perfect, polished works of art. We're looking for budding authors who will improve and gain confidence with time and practice. 99

How can teachers keep track of what kids are writing?

Participating in the writing menu is a privilege. Kids will be asked to govern themselves, make wise choices, stay on task, and produce a body of work. They will be working on several projects during the next few weeks.

After looking at all the choices on the writing menu, giving these careful consideration, and talking to their parents, kids will fill out and sign a contract before starting the writing menu. The contract is an agreement of what a student is going to attempt to accomplish over the next several weeks and signifies a commitment. The teacher keeps a copy and the student keeps a copy. This way the teacher has a written record of each child's direction and can knowledgeably encourage them to keep on task.

Must a contract be fulfilled?

As with any contract, there are instances and reasons why some contracts won't be fulfilled. Contracts are primarily used to keep kids focused during the period of time the class is working on a particular writing menu. While some projects may be attempted and not finished, points are awarded for finished work only. You will set standards of how much work you will require from each student during a writing menu and how many points will be awarded. Additional points can be awarded for fulfilling a contract, exemplary behavior, extra work, presentation, special effects, props, costumes, publishing, etc.

What will take place during the next few weeks?

Each day students will work on their various projects during the daily writing workshop time. Their goal is to complete projects to the best of their creative efforts. High achievers will be able to finish more projects or longer ones.

At the end of several weeks, on an agreed-upon date, all projects are due. You might want to stagger the due dates throughout a week so you don't have every-thing coming in at once. Students will be assessed and rewarded according to what they have accomplished. Praise those who have stayed on task and have been productive. Let each student present one of her projects to the class and share new information she has learned about a subject she is studying.

Writing Menu Contract

Starting Date_____ Due Date_____

I am contracting to WORK on the following writing projects:

Appetizers_____

_____

Main Courses (must have at least one)_____

_____

_____

Desserts_____

_____

_____

I understand that my job is to use my time wisely, stay on task, work independently, and display considerate behavior. I will ask for help if I need it, be of service to others, and work to the best of my abilities. My goals are to produce good writing, earn as many points as possible, and teach the class new knowledge.

Signed:_____

Date: _____

seal
of
completion

Witness:_____

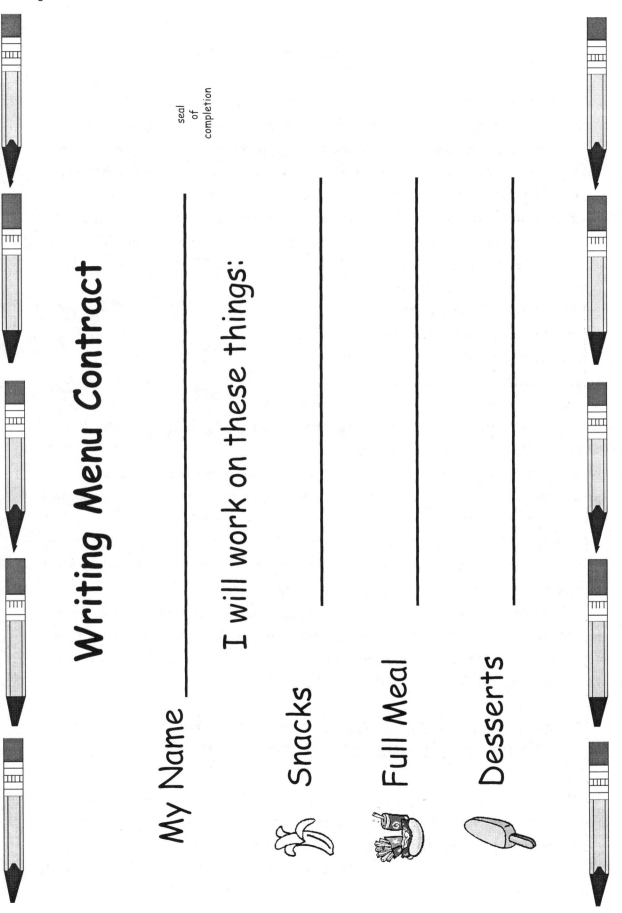

Writing Menu Contract

My Name _____

I will work on these things:

seal of completion

Snacks

Full Meal

Desserts

How can parents help?

Parents are a vital link in the learning chain. Most of them have their child's best interest at heart and want to see him succeed. Typically, they're used to seeing papers come home often and are looking for things like high grades, proper spelling, neat handwriting, etc. Enlisting the help of parents is a key component to making writing menus successful for the kids in your class.

✓ **INFORM** - Send a letter to parents telling them all about writing menus. An example is included for you on page 41. Giving them all the information in writing is a first step to convincing parents. Try to anticipate and answer all questions in advance to stave off confusion.

✓ **INVOLVE** - Invite parents for an evening of writing. Put them through the paces of a mini-writing menu. Provide writing supplies, colored paper, magazine pictures, scissors, markers, etc. Encourage all parents to experience writing, revising, publishing, and presenting just as their children will be doing in class.

✓ **EDUCATE** - Give parents copies of the target skills list, writing handout sheets, sample menus, examples of great student writing, the titles of books to read, and any other resources you have that might be helpful.

✓ **ENLIST** - Let parents know how vital they are in ensuring their child's success. Elicit pledges of support, encouragement, interest, volunteering, supplies, setting aside a special uninterrupted writing time at home, etc.

✓ **REMIND** - Wanting your child to be a success is a natural desire of every parent. Our goal is for parents to be involved, to be informed, and to encourage their child to write and enhance writing projects at home. However, parents need to be reminded NOT TO DO THEIR CHILD'S WORK.

How much time should students have to make their decisions about the writing menu?

Once the menus are planned and introduced, let kids have a number of days to consider their choices before signing a contract. It is a good idea to discuss the menu choices as a class, show examples of creative projects from previous years, and let kids discuss their final selections with their parents. You might choose to have parents sign the contract as a sign of involvement and validation.

Dear Parents,

Our class will be participating in a new type of writing workshop during the next four weeks. Instead of one writing assignment and one time frame to complete it in, there will be many from which children can choose.

The new system, called Writing Menus, will help students write about things we are studying in class and topics that interest them. They will also learn to make some of their own decisions and to write with purpose. Students will be able to choose writing projects about the topics we are studying in class from a special "menu" of selections. I am enclosing a copy for you to see. Please read and discuss it with your child. Also, please become familiar with the student contract and point sheets.

I hope you see an increased interest in writing at home these next few weeks. In addition to writing in class, I am encouraging my students to work on some aspects of their projects at home. This could involve writing, rewriting, illustrations, props, costumes, practicing, or working on the computer. Some good ways to help your child work independantly at home are:

- ✓ Showing interest
- ✓ Not doing his work
- ✓ Answering questions
- ✓ Respecting his choices
- ✓ Encouraging his efforts
- ✓ Giving positive feedback
- ✓ Providing a quiet, organized place
- ✓ Setting aside a special writing time
- ✓ Allowing him to work at his own level

Writing Menus have been designed to help your child become an independent, creative, enthusiastic writer. Reminder: we're not looking for perfect, polished works of art at this point. We're looking for budding authors who will improve and gain confidence with time and practice.

CHAPTER FIVE
Payday: The Point System

A point system for a writing menu is optional. We live in a merit-based society: athletics, competitions, contests, GPAs, salaries, bonuses. Kids love being rewarded and validated for their efforts. They also enjoy working toward pre-set goals and tracking improvement. Through managing their time wisely and producing a body of work from the writing menu, writers can be awarded a flexible number of points. The points might be linked to letter grades (if need be), tangible validations, privileges, or a combination of these. Kids only compete with themselves.

Just as in a real-life job situation, some tasks require more effort than others and therefore are rewarded accordingly. More work produced equals more points. Better work equals more points. Creativity equals more points. Extra effort equals more points. Lackadaisical attempts, wasting time, or sloppy, slipshod writing equal fewer points. Kids soon learn that hard work has practical merits.

How are points assigned to writing projects?

Each writing project from the menu is pre-assigned a value of points. Any number of factors can influence the amount of points per project:

* The amount of time required to complete a project
* Special factors such as research, drawing, props, costumes, etc.
* Writing skills required to complete the project
* Performing or presenting the finished project
* The level and abilities of your students

First of all, assign an escalating scale of points to each project, based on the time and skill it would take to complete it to satisfaction. For example:

✓ Write a list of juicy color words in the Red Family = 1 point per word
✓ List inventions of the past 100 years = 1 point per invention
✓ Write a limerick about a zoo animal = 5 points per limerick
✓ Write a one-paragraph restaurant review= 8 points per review
✓ Write a two-minute speech about school safety = 30 points per speech
✓ Present your original school-safety speech = 10 points per presentation
✓ Write a story that takes place on a mysterious island = 40 points per story

✓ Write a play about pioneers traveling West = 40 points per play

✓ Present your original play = 20 points per presentation

✓ Take pictures of a community helper and write a three-paragraph photo essay about the importance of his job = 40 points per essay

✓ Draw a treasure map and write "clues" about where the treasure is buried and how it can be found = 20 points per map and clues

These points represent revised, edited, completed projects. The number you've assigned indicates *possible points*. In order to receive the full number of points for a project, students will have to complete it to your specifications. Projects that don't live up to your expectations may receive fewer points. Projects that are exceptional and have added more than your requirements might receive more points. Projects that are attempted and not completed may receive no points at all. The point system keeps kids focused on revising, editing, and finishing writing.

How do you develop a point-value system?

After you've assigned points to each project, estimate an *average amount of points* most of your students could earn in a given day, taking into consideration the amount of time you've set aside for writing workshop. At this juncture you might want to try a sample week and see how many points your students earn on average. For example, it might be somewhere in the neighborhood of 15 points earned per day. Eager beavers might be able earn more than 15 points per day and, at the same time, a few students may earn fewer. Get a classroom average.

Next, determine the *least amount of points* that would be acceptable to earn in a given day. For example, you might decide most of your third graders could earn at *least* 10 points per day during your 45-minute writing workshop. (Keep in mind that this is just an assumption of the *least* amount of points that would be acceptable to earn.)

Multiply these totals times the number of days for a writing menu:

At least 10 points per day x 20 days =   200 points minimum

An average of 15 points per day x 20 days =   300 points average

Use these figures to determine a point-value system based on the number of points a student might earn each day times the number of days. The point system is not to foster competition, but to encourage **self-evaluation** and **goal setting**.

How and when are the points tallied?

After completing their various projects from the writing menu, students will ready their work to be turned in to the teacher to be assessed. They will help with some of the preliminary tallying by recording their accomplishments on their writing menu point sheets (Page 46). During a staggered period of days, the teacher will assess each student's body of work and award points according to the standards specified earlier. Ideally the teacher will then schedule an assessment appointment with each writer to discuss his work.

A student is awarded all or part of the possible points for each project. Additional points can be awarded for using specific target skills, using spelling and vocabulary words, giving a presentation to the class, etc. Bonus points can be special rewards for any number of exceptional behaviors.

What does the point-value system stand for?

It wouldn't make too much sense to have a point-value system if it didn't represent some sort of validation students can strive for. Points can be used to help teachers determine a writing grade if one is called for. Grades don't really represent an accurate picture when it comes to a subjective discipline such as writing and they seem to conjure up a negative connotation. However, some teachers are still asked to give writing grades, and points can be used to arrive at a logical grade. Come up with a grading scale that works for you and reflects the abilities of your students. The following is just one possible example of a scale:

Points Earned:			Optional Letter Grade:
371 and above			A+
361	-	370	A
351	-	360	A-
341	-	350	B+
331	-	340	B
321	-	330	B-
311	-	320	C+
301	-	310	C
291	-	300	C-
281	-	290	D+
271	-	280	D
261	-	270	D-
260 and below			F

In addition to or instead of grades, points can represent some sort of validation, such as spending points in the classroom store, earning privileges, or a "credit card" system to redeem small prizes, school supplies, computer time, homework passes, etc. Kids look forward to Pay Day and the privileges their rewards evoke. Pull out all the stops and make this a big deal in your classroom.

2001-91

Date

PAY TO _____ $ _____

1 Writing Menu Bonus Buck _____ DOLLARS

✂ *copy and cut apart*

2001-91

Date

PAY TO _____ $ _____

5 Writing Menu Bonus Bucks _____ DOLLARS

2001-91

Date

PAY TO _____ $ _____

10 Writing Menu Bonus Bucks _____ DOLLARS

☆☆☆   # Writing Menu Point Sheet   ☆☆☆

Name_____ Date_____

Writing projects completed:	Points Possible:	Points Earned:
_____	_____	_____ ☆
_____	_____	_____ ☆
_____	_____	_____ ☆
_____	_____	_____ ☆
_____	_____	_____ ☆
_____	_____	_____ ☆

Target skills I have used: Vocabulary and spelling words:

_____   _____

_____   _____

_____   _____

_____   _____

_____   _____

_____Points:_____ ☆   _____Points:_____ ☆

Knowledge I have taught the class through my writing projects:

_____

_____

_____

_____Points:_____ ☆

Bonus Points: ☆ ☆ ☆

_____ ☆ **Helping others**

_____ ☆ **Creativity**

_____ ☆ **Working independently**

_____ ☆ **Considerate behavior**

_____ ☆ **Presentation**

Earned Points: _____ ☆

Bonus Points: _____ ☆

Total Score: _____ ★

Name_____ Date_____

I have earned points for:

★ Putting my name on my paper _____

★ Brainstorming ideas before I write _____

★ Following directions _____

★ Using a spelling word in my writing _____

★ Using a vocabulary word in my writing _____

★ Sounding out words on my own _____

★ Giving my writing a title _____

★ Starting sentences with capital letters _____

★ Ending sentences with punctuation _____

★ Adding details to my writing _____

★ Drawing pictures to go with my writing _____

★ Answering questions about my writing _____

★ Sharing from the Author's Chair _____

★ Working independently _____

★ Helping another child with his writing _____

★ Completing my work _____

TOTAL POINTS: _____

★ ★ ★ ★ ★ ★ ★

CHAPTER SIX
The Writing Menu Layout

After you've planned a variety of writing projects that reflect the units, topics, and subjects you will be teaching in your academic areas, it's time to put them all together in a writing menu format. Writing menus can be simple, such as a few typed pages, or elaborate, such as the ones you'll find in this chapter. At any rate, be creative. Pay attention to detail. Using graphics, slogans, witticisms, and special effects will add to the excitement and fun. Kids respond to anything special.

Keeping each menu on a computer disk will help you avoid doing the same work year after year as you plan future menus. Experiment with the format that works best for you and your students, adding and changing as you wish. You may use any of the examples or graphics included in this chapter or design your own to reflect school names, mascots, and colors. The creation of your writing menus will be a work in progress, a metamorphosis, and you can add fresh ideas as needed.

What needs to be on the cover?

We do judge books by their covers, don't we? The writing menu cover is the first thing your kids will see, so it should be designed to catch their attention. Eye-catching. Dazzling. Fun! Using that sparkling wit of yours, come up with a funny name for your menu and watch kids go wild. Now's the time to experiment with those crazy fonts and graphics you've always wanted to try. Stumped? Involve the art teacher, a team of creative parents, or the school computer wizard to help.

What needs to be on the information page?

The information page explains how long the writing menu will be used, how to make choices of writing projects, the point system, and other key information. You will explain these things in detail, of course, but this page serves as a reminder for students and a guide for parents. If your information page works well, it can be used again and again on future menus so kids can get used to the same rules and guidelines. Several information pages are included in this chapter to help you in your planning. If you are using a point system, it is a good idea to give kids the point-value chart along with the information page so they can plan their choices and finish their projects accordingly.

MENU

Abraham Lincoln Elementary
Presents...

Mrs. Claymore's Corner Cafe

Culinary delights to
tingle the tongue...
enthrall the eyes...
stimulate the senses...

FRIES

Step one

Read the menu carefully. Spend some time thinking about the projects that sound good to you. Read the contract sheet.

Step two

Choose the projects you want to work on from start to finish. Write the names of the projects on the contract sheet. Choose a witness, then both of you sign the contract.

Step Three

Begin working on your writing projects. Follow the directions for each project. Do your very best to be creative and make your writing interesting and informative. Points will be awarded for creativity and content.

Step Four

Revise your writing several times. Ask other class members to read your writing and give you suggestions. Add target skills and writers' tricks to make your writing more enjoyable for the reader.

Step Five

After you finish writing and revising, make your work more creative by adding pictures, photos, an illustration, models, maps, props, or costumes. You may work on these at home and in your spare time.

Step Six

Practice presenting at least one of your writing projects to the class. Plan to teach the other kids some interesting information through your presentation. Impress us!

Step Seven

Prepare to turn in all finished, edited writing projects by the due date. Fill out the point sheet and organize your work into a neat packet of writing.

WRITING WORKSHOP MENU
INFORMATION PAGE

Welcome to the Crazy Kid Cafe Menu. It's just like choosing your favorite foods in a restaurant. Each author will be able to choose writing projects he'd like to work on during the next four weeks. The choice is yours!

Each project is worth points. The number of projects you complete and how well you do them will determine the amount of points you earn! Only finished projects will earn points. Work hard.

At the end of the four weeks, your writing grade will be partially based on these points. In addition, you can buy prizes from our class store with your points. Cool! You may choose from

any of the categories. You may work on as many projects as you like as long as you finish them. Some kids might choose a long project. Other kids will choose several shorter ones.

Look over the menu and see what appeals to you. You have several days to make up your mind.

Each day during writing workshop you will need to work on something the entire time. If you get stuck, need help, or have a few extra minutes, work on a short project for the time being. Don't waste time by just sitting. Real authors budget their time wisely.

Spend class time writing so we can help each other revise and edit our work. You may work on illustrations, props, and costumes at home or in class after you've finished writing.

At the end of the four weeks you may present some portion of your work to the class. We are depending on you to teach us important information through your writing projects. Make your projects interesting, funny, exciting, informative, amazing, charming, touching, or curious.

The Crazy Kid Cafe Menu is a new and creative way to write about things we are studying. Have fun searching the menu and making your choices. Bon Appetit!

The Crazy Kid Cafe

APPETIZERS

Fried Cheese Sticks - Onomatopoeia are words that name special sounds such as snap, crackle, and pop. Make a list of onomatopoeia words you might hear in the tropical rain forest.

1 point possible for every 5 words

Nachos - Write a List of Details of things you would find in a marine-biology lab.

1 point possible for every 5 words

Buffalo Wings - Draw one of the mammals of North America we are studying. Label the parts of the mammal.

5 points possible for labeled drawing

Blooming Onion - A simile is a phrase that compares two things using the words "like" or "as." Write some new similes, using descriptive, juicy words.

2 points possible per simile

Shrimp Cocktail - Write a sentence about a specific way we use math to help us at home. Be sure to include who, what, when, where, why, and how.

2 points possible per sentence

  ## MAIN COURSES

Steak and French Fries - Pretend you are a slave living in the South before the Civil War. You want to go North to freedom on the underground railroad. Write a diary of one week in your life telling about your escape, who you travel with, what you eat, and some exciting things that happen. Don't leave out any details!

20 points possible

Fried Chicken Platter - You are a research scientist in the rain forest of Panama. Write a letter inviting a class of school children to spend a week with you in the jungle. Tell them what they will see, what they will do each day, where they will stay, and what they should bring.

10 points possible

Fish and Chips - Interview a person who works at our school: principal, nurse, cafeteria worker, janitor, librarian, etc. Write a report describing his job, how he helps our school, what questions you asked, and how he answered. Take a photo to go along with your report or draw an illustration.

15 points possible

Fajitas - Write a "how to" paragraph about one of the chores you do at home. List all the steps in order and remember to use transition words. Take a photo of each step or draw illustrations. Make a poster of your paragraph and pictures.
20 points possible

Neckbones and Greens - Pretend the governor has asked you to write a song about living in the state of Florida. You may use a familiar tune if you want to. Be sure to write about all the things that make Florida such a special place to live. Write several verses and a chorus. Practice, and present your song to the class.
20 points possible

Gator Pot Pie - Write a story about a camping trip in the backwoods of Florida. Set the scene by describing where you camp and the other characters who are with you. Introduce a "problem" that will make us laugh or scare the daylights out of us. Develop a story that kids will enjoy reading. Draw illustrations or use computer clip art to illustrate the action. Ask five students to read your rough draft and make suggestions that will improve your story. Revise several times using a different color of ink each day you. Copy or type the final draft and publish it as a book other kids will want to read.
25 points possible

  **DESSERTS**

Banana Split - Draw a picture of a famous person. Write a few sentences giving clues to the person's identity. See how many class members can guess!
5 points possible

Hot Fudge Sundae - Cut out a picture of a car, truck, or motorcycle you'd like to own. Call or visit the local dealer and find out as much information about it as you can. Write a few sentences and mount them underneath the picture. Where could you buy one? How much would it cost? What colors and styles are there to choose from? What features make this vehicle special? Why would you choose it?
5 points possible

Fresh Fruit Platter - Make a clay-dough model of an animal you would find in the tropical rain forest. Write an information paragraph about the animal to go along with your display.
5 points possible

Baked Alaska - Pretend you are stranded alone on an island. Write a message you could put in a bottle. Tell us how you ended up on the island, what you're doing for food and shelter, and a message to your family.
5 points possible

Writing Menu

My Name _____

 Snacks

1. Draw a picture of a clown. Write two sentences about the clown.

   5 points each picture

2. Cut out pictures of fruits and vegetables. Paste them on a piece of colored paper and write the name of each fruit or vegetable below the picture.

   5 points each picture

3. Write pairs of rhyming words like: red * bed, bee * knee, pay * day, and sink * pink.

   1 point each pair

4. Draw five ice cream cones and color the ice cream a different color on each cone. Write the names of the colors.

   1 point each cone

5. Write the name of a person in our class. Write two sentences about that person.

   2 points each person

 Full Meals

6. Write a story about one of the famous Americans we've been studying. Tell about his life. Tell why he is an important person. Draw a picture to go with your story.

   15 points each story

7. Think of a person who works at our school who is a helper. Pretend you are that person. Write some things that will tell the children in our room about your job.

   15 points each person

8. Choose one of the pictures on the table. All the pictures were taken during Mrs. Forney's life. Ask her questions about the picture you choose. Now write a story about what is going on in the picture. Share your story and picture with the class.

    15 points each story

9. Think of a favorite book you've read. Write about the book. Tell us why you liked the book. Tell some things you learned by reading this good book. Make a clay model to go with your writing.

    15 points each book

 # Desserts

10. Make up a song about Betsy Ross sewing our country's flag. Practice your song, then sing it for the class.

    5 points each song

11. Write a poem about an animal that lives at the zoo. Don't forget to make it funny!

    5 points each poem

12. Write an e-mail message to the President of the United States. Tell him what you think about our country.

    5 points each e-mail

CHAPTER SEVEN
More Writing Menu Selections

Now that you've seen some actual writing menus, more examples of menu selections might be helpful. As you plan your own menus, you can choose some of these or create your own. Make sure you've taught a particular genre and kids have had several chances to practice before introducing it on a writing menu. The selections in this chapter, while not claiming to be all-inclusive, will give you a sampling of topics, genres, and formats.

United States History

1. Consider what it would feel like to see the New World for the very first time as you sail with Christopher Columbus on the Pinta, Nina, or Santa Maria. Write an imaginary, one-week journal of things you would see and experience in the year 1492

2. Write an imaginary interview with George Washington Carver about his amazing discoveries that have helped so many people.

3. Tell the story of a pioneer family's adventure as they cross the Great Plains to build a new homestead and establish a new life far, far away from home.

4. Draw a "Wanted" poster about a famous outlaw and write a brief history of his life to go under the picture.

5. Write ten Jeopardy questions and answers about the life of a famous American. Try to stump the audience!

6. Imagine you are able to write a letter that can be sent back in time to a famous American. Warn him about something that will happen so perhaps he can change the course of history.

7. Pretend you were a slave who had secretly learned to read and write even though you had been forbidden to do so. Write a letter of thanks to President Abraham Lincoln for freeing you and all the other slaves during the Civil War.

8. Write a dramatic story about the men who built the great railroads of America. Be sure to tell us about some of the terrible dangers and hardships they faced.

9. Read a book about your favorite period in American history. Write a book review and tell some important things that happened during this period. Make us want to read and enjoy the book as you did.

10. Pretend you are a great army general during World War II. Write a speech you might give to the men who will fight in your army just before a big battle. Inspire them with your words and convince them they are helping our country.

11. You are a newspaper reporter who travels back to the year 1776 to witness the signing of the Declaration of Independence. Now write a factual newspaper report about what you saw and how the course of history is going to be changed.

12. Imagine you are part of the California Gold Rush. Write a letter home to your wife and family telling about your adventures and success searching for gold.

13. Write a humorous but factual song about the Boston Tea Party so the students in your class will never forget this important event in history.

14. During the past 200 years, many immigrants have come to America by ship to start a new life. Write a diary of a kid who endures the hardships on board ship and then sees the Statue of Liberty for the first time.

15. Using story-poems like "Casey at the Bat" and "The Highwayman" as examples, write an exciting story-poem about the building of the Panama Canal.

16. Imagine you are an injured soldier who has been fighting in the Civil War. You are now dying in a hospital far away from your family. Write your final letter to them telling about your injuries and the horrors of war.

17. Pretend you are the first kid to travel into outer space on the space shuttle. Write a journal about your training at NASA, the shuttle flight, and your great experience in space.

18. If you could design a new stamp for the United States Post Office, whose face would you put on it and why? What has this person done for America? Why have you chosen this person?

19. Imagine your teacher has been working secretly on a time machine and offers you a chance to go back in history for one day. Where would you choose to go and what year would it be? What would happen while you were there? How would you get back to the present time?

20. Voting for our president is an important responsibility for every citizen. If kids were allowed to vote, what kinds of qualities would you look for in a president and how would these qualities benefit our country?

Inventors and Explorers

1. Draw a comic-book story about the Wright brothers and their first airplane flight at Kitty Hawk. Move the story forward with captions or dialogue and keep us on the edge of excitement!

2. Travel back in time to the laboratory of Thomas Edison. Write a short play about his discovery of the electric light bulb.

3. Write a fictionalized television interview with Hernando de Soto as he and his men discover the Mississippi River in the year 1541. Ask important questions and allow him to describe his years of hardship and exploration.

4. Make a list of 50 important inventions you and your family use around your house to make life easier. Which would be the hardest to do without?

5. Write an advertisement for one of Henry Ford's Model T cars. Keep in mind that most people had never seen or ridden in a car before this time.

6. Build a homemade kite and tie a metal key to it. Now write a speech about Benjamin Franklin's discovery of electricity. Using the kite as an interesting prop, present your speech to the class so they will always remember this historic event.

...Inventors and Explorers

7. Some scientists consider the wheel to be the most useful invention. Write a paragraph about the many ways wheels are useful to your own life.

8. Amelia Earhart dazzled Americans during the 1930s by sailing around the world in her "flying ship." Write a checklist for her of important things she needs to check before she leaves and supplies she should pack aboard her airplane.

9. Cut out pictures of 50 things that have been invented since you were born. Write a descriptive, informative sentence to go with each picture.

10. Many simple machines don't need electricity. Write a list of 25 simple machines that we use almost every day.

11. Imagine you have found a phone number that will magically connect you to Alexander Graham Bell at his workshop in 1876, the year he first patented the telephone. Write an imaginary conversation between you and Mr. Bell. Be sure to tell him about all the cool telephone inventions we have today.

12. Inventions help our lives. Write a story about something imaginary that you invent that every kid wants to own. Make sure you tell us how your successful invention rockets you to fame and fortune.

13. It has been said that "Necessity is the mother of invention." Write a paragraph about something that has not been invented yet that would solve an important "need" and be of great use to the world.

14. The microscope was an important invention that allowed doctors and scientists to see bacteria and other germs that caused infections and patient deaths. How has the world been improved by the invention of the microscope?

15. One of the most important inventions of the past 1,000 years is the printing press. How was the world different before the printing press? How was news spread and important events remembered?

16. Imagine you are a future student at your elementary school 100 years from

Inventors and Explorers...

now. Write a story of the awesome inventions that have made life so different for kids and teachers in the future.

17. Write a radio drama about an important discovery in the life of an inventor. Practice the drama with a few other "actors" and present it to your class.

Animals and Pets

1. Most pets are dependent on their owners for food and care. Choose an interesting pet and write a mini instruction manual for taking care of him. Teach the rest of us to be loving, responsible owners.

2. Zoos are fascinating places to visit, but you wouldn't want to be locked in one by mistake overnight. Unfortunately, that's exactly what happens to you. Write a story telling about your great, overnight zoo adventure!

3. Pretend you are an animal who is being raised in a laboratory. You've never known what it feels like to be free or live in the wild. Write a daring adventure story about a boy who sets you free and takes you back to the wild to join others of your kind. Make sure there's an exciting ending to your story!

4. You are playing kickball at the playground in your neighborhood and someone kicks the ball underneath some bushes. While looking for the ball you spot a large, peculiar egg. There is no nest in sight and you have no clue as to what kind of egg it is. You take the egg home and put it in your dirty-clothes hamper to keep it warm. Write a story telling what happens to the egg, what hatches from it, and what kind of adventure follows.

5. Take pictures of your pet doing all the things you love best. Mount them on poster board and write a short explanation paragraph to go under each picture.

6. Imagine you and your dog go to a grassy field to watch a hot-air-balloon crew get their balloon ready for takeoff. When no one is looking, the two of you climb into the basket just to see what it's like inside. The ropes accidentally loosen and

suddenly you float high up into the air. Write a story telling what happens, where you go, and how you get back to the ground safely.

7. Write a story about swimming with a group of dolphins one magical day when suddenly you begin to understand their language and they can understand yours.

8. Some people are cruel to animals. What can we do to protect animals so people will treat them with kindness and respect?

9. Pretend you are one of the many unusual, exotic animals we've studied. Write 10 "guess who" clues about yourself and challenge the class to guess who you are.

10. Draw a comic book about the adventures of Cyberdog, a dog who is really a computer genius and goes online the minute his human family leaves for work and school everyday.

11. Write a play about the animals in a mall pet store. Each evening, when the manager closes up the store, he thinks the animals will be asleep soon, but they let each other out of their cages and have wild parties.

12. Write a fictional newspaper report about a pet parrot who has gotten lost. Tell how he got away, his background, information about the family who owns him, and, of course, a reward.

Tropical Rain Forests

1. Write a letter to the head of a country that has an important tropical rain forest. Convince her of the importance of saving the rain forest from destruction. List ways she can save the forest and the benefits for the entire world.

2. Pretend you are a scientist in a tropical rain forest. Write a diary of some unusual things that have happened to you this past week as you explore the jungle, its animals, and plants. Give us specific details that happen on each day, and be sure to take us on some wild adventures!

...Tropical Rain Forests

3. Write a chapter book about two best friends who win a science contest and get to spend the summer with a world famous scientist in the tropical rain forest. Tell about the amazing but dangerous mission they have.

4. Imagine you are a real-estate agent for a tropical rain forest. Your job is to try to get animals that used to live in the rain forest to come back again. Describe the lush forest, the trees and vegetation, and tell the animals about the "new and improved" rain forest they will enjoy.

5. Write a list of 25 animals that live in the rain forest and a descriptive sentence about each one. Draw a picture of one animal you consider fascinating.

6. Living as a scientist in a tropical rain forest would be tough, grueling work. Pretend you are just such a scientist and in the middle of an afternoon downpour, you are fed up, frustrated, and generally disgusted. Write a list entitled "Reasons I Never Want to Live in a Rain Forest Again!"

7. Many primitive tribes of people live in lush rain forests throughout the world. Some are living like they did thousands of years ago. Some people think they are better left alone. Others think they should have the benefits of modern society. What do you think? Write a paragraph giving your opinion and support it with as many specific reasons as you can.

8. Plan a field trip for your class to a tropical rain forest. Tell about the specific location you will be visiting, how you will get there, supplies that will be needed when you get there, and what you will see and learn.

9. Write and produce a commercial for a new television program called "Jungle Trek" that will take place deep in the tropical rain forest. Practice your best "TV voice" so you can audio tape or video tape your commercial. Teach the class lots of interesting information about the rain forest in your two-minute commercial. Tease the audience with clues about the opening story for the series. Be sure to use sound effects, pictures, stuffed animals, costumes, or props to make your jungle commercial seem as real as possible.

Family Relationships

1. Most members of families help out with chores. Describe the one chore you absolutely hate to do and convince us why it's the worst chore in the world.

2. Moms do lots of nice things to take care of their kids. If your mother was sick and had to stay in bed for a week, how would you take care of her?

3. Why do brothers and sisters always fight, anyway? Tell about your relationship with a brother or sister and describe how you play and live together. What are some good ways for the two of you to learn to get along better? Why would this be important for your whole family?

4. Being a good parent is a tough job. What are some important things parents need to do in order to set good examples for their children?

5. If you were going to write your autobiography right now, describe three events you think are the most important things that have happened in your life so far. Be sure to tell how these events have helped shape you into the person you are.

6. Write a story about finding an old family photo album in your attic. Most of the pictures are of your ancestors who lived a long time ago. When you tap any one of the pictures three times with both thumbs you are magically transported back to the time and setting of that photo. Describe one of the photos and tell the great adventure that happens when you go back in time to the scene in the photo.

7. Ask your mother, father, grandmother or grandfather to tell you a story about when they were kids. Write the story for the class to enjoy, remembering to add all the details and dialogue that make stories so interesting to hear.

8. Every single one of us has a rich heritage. Interview some of your oldest family members and write down your "family tree." Be sure to include information about your culture, ethnic background, your family's religion, famous people who are related to you, and how your ancestors originally came to this country.

9. Write an imaginary family-advice column for kids called, *Dear Henrietta*. Write

...Family Relationships

some questions kids might ask about families. Answer their questions with the best advice you can think of. You may make your column funny but be courteous as well.

10. Plan a perfect Saturday for your family - stuff to do, places to go. The only trick is you can't spend more than $10 the entire day. Where would you go? What would you do? How would this be an ideal trip for each member of your family?

11. Write 10 one-sentence "thank you" notes to members of your family for special things they've done for you. Hide them around your house in places where they'll be found by your family members.

12. Make a greeting card on the computer for an older family member, perhaps one who lives far away. Ask each member of your family to write a sentence or two of personal greeting. Add your own greeting, address the envelope, and mail it.

13. Ask your family to help you create and bury (or store) a "Family Time Capsule" of special articles and photos that tell about your family life. Agree to open the capsule 25 years from now on a special date.

14. Ask your family to visit a cemetery where someone famous is buried. Take some large sheets of paper and dark, colored chalk. Make a "rubbing" of the front of the gravestone or marker. Find out all you can about the person who is buried there and write a short biography about her. Share your writing with the class.

15. Go for a nature walk with your family. Take old blankets, a magnifying glass, a flashlight, and binoculars. Spread your blanket under some shady trees. Using the tools you brought, examine plants, animals, insects, and other living things at close range. Record your findings. You may take photographs, if you like.

16. Interview your family members and ask them to describe their favorite meals. Plan a supper menu for an entire week that lists specific foods that are family favorites. Try to plan some things that will be pleasing to everyone. Be sure to include something from each of the food groups.

17. The world has changed quite a bit during the past 25 years. Interview your parents or grandparents about what life was like when they were your age. Ask them about changes they've seen. Write an essay about some major ways the world has changed.

Community Helpers

1. Some people think it would be a good thing for kids to have paid jobs. If you were able to get a job in your community, describe the kind of work that would be interesting and fun for you. What salary do you think would be fair payment? What special training would you need?

2. Pretend you have been asked to "shadow" a professional person for one day as he does his job. Describe the person you shadow, how you help with his job, and the adventures that could happen during your day together.

3. Being a policeman is a dangerous but rewarding job. Write your own version of a T.V. show called, "Police Force One," and take us on a wild police adventure that helps make your community a safer place to live.

4. Would it be fun to plan a brand new city, designed by you? Plan and design a city, give your city a name, draw a poster-size drawing of the city's layout. Add all of the important features such as businesses, schools, hospitals, etc. Write a brochure about your city that tells interesting historical facts and invites people to move to your city. Add features that would make this a desirable place to live.

5. Sometimes it doesn't seem fair that the very workers who risk their lives to help members of our community are paid low salaries. Interview a policeman or a fireman. Compare their salary to other community helpers. Write a report on your research and make suggestions of how we can reward and honor these important workers who we call in emergency situations.

6. Make a chart of community helpers in our city. Find out their names and what jobs they are responsible for. Describe the training they have to go through to learn their skill and how their job is a help to local citizens.

School and Education

1. If you could bury three important things in a time capsule for school children to open in 100 years, what three things would you bury and why would you choose those things? What would they teach children of the future about our culture?

2. If a foreign student came to the United States for one month to see what America was like and you could plan his trip, what are three locations you would want him to see? Describe each of these locations and why you chose them.

3. Schools are planned and run by adults. Most kids wish they could change some things about their schools. What would you change and how would things be better for kids and teachers?

4. School bullies usually pick on kids weaker or smaller than they are. Write a story about a bully who learns that threats and violence won't get him his way.

5. What would be the ideal field-trip location for your class if you didn't have to worry about money or distance? Why would this be a good place to visit? Explain what your class would learn by going on this trip.

6. Classrooms are usually run by teachers. Describe how a classroom of the future might work if kids stayed at home and were linked to each other and a teacher by computers. How would things be better that way? What would you miss about not being in a traditional classroom?

7. Sometimes friends ask to copy our homework or give them the answers on a test. Explain how you feel about cheating. Does it make any difference when it comes to helping your friends?

8. How are you going to prepare for the future you want for yourself? What education or experiences will you need to get ready for success? How will you keep focused on this goal so you can achieve your dream?

9. Write a play about some kids who get into trouble at school. Be sure to create an interesting problem and a workable solution. Choose actors to play the parts you have written. Practice the play and present it to the class.

Black History

1. Dr. Martin Luther King, Jr.'s dream was for all races to live together in harmony, without prejudice. Explain some things we can all do to create racial harmony in our country.

2. One of the darkest periods in our history was when slaves were owned by greedy plantation owners and forced to work all their lives in cruel bondage. Write a poem from the point of view of a slave child. What deep emotions would you feel when you saw your own family having to struggle through such hardships?

3. Rosa Parks changed the course of history by refusing to give up her seat on the bus. Write a play of the conversation that might have taken place on the bus that important day when Mrs. Parks stood up for her rights. Through dialogue, show the reader how everyone on the bus felt.

4. Write a diary as if you are a runaway slave trying to make it to freedom through the underground railroad. Tell what happens each night as you and other runaways run for your lives from the bounty hunters who try to capture you.

5. Listen to and study a selection of music written and played by an African-American musician. Write a report about the person's life and find out all you can about why he chose that particular type of music. Play your selection for the class and share your findings about the musician's biographical background.

6. Make a poster with pictures of famous African-Americans and their valuable contributions to history and the world. Write a few informative sentences under each picture that describe what you find in your research.

7. African-American foods and cooking have enriched the diet we eat in America. Find a recipe for an African-American dish. Cook this at home and bring samples for the class to try. Explain how you made the dish and its historical background.

8. Interview an older African-American. Ask about unusual customs and stories from his childhood. Ask questions and take careful notes. Present your findings in a report using the question and answer format. If possible, invite your subject to be a guest in your classroom to share stories and personal experiences.

Kids

1. We've had many natural disasters in our own country and all over the world. Usually it's the adults who help the survivors. If a team of specially trained kids was formed to help in emergency situations, what skills would be important for them to learn? If you were on the team, which job would you want to do? How could a team of kids help in an emergency?

2. Having great friends is one of the neat things about being a kid. Think of someone special. Explain why this person is your close friend and why you like him.

3. If the President of the United States invited you to meet with a special group for a day to discuss the needs of children in America, what are some things you might suggest or discuss?

4. Everyone has to make choices in life. What do you think are the three most important choices you will have to make in your life? Why? What will you have to consider in making these choices?

5. Write an essay about your favorite television program or movie. Give reasons why it is your favorite and support those reasons with many details and examples. Convince the reader that he should want to watch this program.

6. Sometimes adults say, "You're just a kid," because they might have forgotten that kids can make a difference in the world. Think of some ways kids can make their community and the world better places. Now write an essay about ways kids can make a difference.

7. In your opinion, in which season are there more fun things to do? Write a five-paragraph essay describing your choice of season. Support your opinion with many facts, details, and examples.

8. Many kids look up to some type of hero, either an athlete, an actor, or a music star. Do you think these public heroes have a responsibility to set a good example? If you agree, explain how they could set good examples for the millions of kids who want to be just like them. If you disagree, tell us how why you feel the way you do and convince us why your opinion is right.

Math

1. Write a song about earning and saving money. Use math terms in the lyrics.

2. Plan a hot-air balloon trip from your school to London, England. Draw the route on a map or a write-on globe. Using an atlas, calculate and record the total number of miles you will travel. Write a travel itinerary for your trip.

3. Ask 10 kids in your class to participate in a "study" you are conducting. Find out exactly how long they were at birth and how tall they are now. How much has each individual grown since birth? Who has grown the tallest? Who was the shortest at birth? Who is the shortest now? Write a report comparing your findings.

4. Write an "owner's guide" about the expenses involved in taking care of a dog for one year. Be sure to include all aspects of the dog's care and calculate the total.

5. Write a sales pitch for a brand new car or truck. Convince your customer that he can afford your vehicle with your creative financial plan and unbeatable price.

Story Starters

1. You are looking through some old books in the attic and find a secret recipe written on an old, old scrap of paper. What is the recipe for? Where did it come from? Who wrote it? Write a story telling what happens when you cook the recipe.

2. Write a story as if you were a passenger on the Titanic the night it sank. Describe the scenes you saw, the emotions you felt, and how you were rescued. No fair using the same exact events in the movie---make up an original story.

3. You have to go to the emergency-room for a minor injury. While you are taking a little nap on the emergency room cart, a nurse mistakes you for another kid and wheels you away to another part of the hospital. Yikes! Write a story about the case of mistaken identity!

4. You and your two best friends are walking along the beach when you spy a floating glass bottle with a message in it. Write a story about the message and the strange adventure it leads to.

...Story Starters

5. Imagine you have a pen pal from a foreign country who you've been writing to for several years. Your pen pal invites you to visit his country, and your parents allow you to go for one week. Write the story of meeting your pen pal. Be sure to tell what his country is like, what foods and customs you discover, and an exciting adventure or two you share with your new friend.

6. Have you ever wondered what it would be like to switch places with someone for a day? You would look and sound like the other person, but inside you would really be you. Write a story about switching places with someone for a day. Be sure to tell us what funny things happen, what mischief you get into, and how you get back to being "you."

7. Write a story about visiting your school 200 years in the future. How has technology changed the way things are done? What cool, new inventions help the students learn and get their work done. How do kids get to school each day?

8. Imagine a space ship lands in the United States of America and the friendly aliens meet with Congress and the President for several weeks. The President finally announces that the aliens would like to invite one elementary school class to visit their planet for a month so that children from both planets can get to know each other and promote peaceful relationships. Your class volunteers to go with the aliens. Write the great adventure that follows.

9. Your class has won a contest that entitles you to a dream field trip, and all your expenses will be paid. You can go anywhere in the world for an entire week. Write a story about where your class goes, exciting things that happen, and how your lives are changed forever by this trip of a lifetime.

10. Tall tales are exaggerated stories that are so unbelievable they make us laugh. Often they are explanations for things we see in nature, such as "How the skunk got his stripe," or "Why birds hatch from eggs." Write a tall tale with a fantastic explanation of something in nature.

11. Suppose you have a secret laboratory in your basement. You and your friends like to create experiments. Write a story about something strange and unusual you

create. What problems do you create and how do you solve them?

12. A limousine pulls up to your school and soon the principal calls your name over the loud speaker. Write a story about who is in the limousine and why you have been called. Where do you go? What happens? How does the story end?

13. Write a fantasy about some computer-game characters that really come to life. Who are they? What happens when they come to life? How are you involved?

14. Write a story about a land where people don't need money to live. Things they need grow on trees or can be found in nature. Other things are free. What is it like to live there? How is a society without money different from ours?

15. Helping people can give us great satisfaction. Imagine you find ten million dollars and decide to keep one million dollars for yourself. You make a promise to help people with the other nine million. Write a story about how you spend the money to help people who really need help. How do you distribute your wealth wisely? How do people react to your incredible generosity? How do you feel?

16. Pretend you are a tick living on a big, shaggy dog. Tell how you got on the dog in the first place, how you look for food, and how the dog reacts to your being there. How do the dog and his owner try to kill you? How do you avoid certain death?

17. Imagine you are a lion cub on the plains of Africa. Your mother, a great lioness, has just been killed by a poacher. Your brother and sister cubs will die unless you stick together and help each other. Write a play about what you do to stay alive after your mother is killed.

18. Write a story about a boy who raises chickens so he can sell the eggs. For a while things go fine: the chickens lay beautiful white eggs. But then one day the boy notices that the eggs are beginning to change....into gold!

19. Write a fairy tale about a land of fun-loving princesses, magical gnomes, talking flowers, fire-breathing dragons, flying carpets, brave heroes, strong horses, wise kings and queens, majestic castles, and knights in shining armor.

Expository Prompts

1. You are an organ instructor at Body Bootcamp. Write an instruction manual for a brand new heart. Tell him what he will be doing each day, how and when to pump blood, and all the information he will need to be a healthy, working heart.

2. You are in a contest to cook the worst recipe imaginable. The trick is you can only use real foods that people eat anyway but you will put them together in weird combinations. Make up a recipe. Tell what ingredients you use, how you would prepare the dish and how it would be served.

3. Machines make our lives simpler. Think of a machine that makes something easier for you. Describe how it works and why it is necessary to your daily life.

4. We need energy to do all the things we like to do during the day. How can we keep our body energy levels high?

5. A friend of yours has been in the hospital for a while recovering from a bad accident. Now your friend is home from the hospital, but he is still weak from being in bed so long. How would you help your friend get back in physical shape so the two of you could go canoeing next summer, which is five months away?

6. It's important to have a plan of action before an emergency occurs. What could your family do to get ready for a hurricane before one arrives? Include some charts, lists, and job assignments for each member of your family.

7. What are some things that change when people get old, and what kind of special needs do older adults have? Why are they important for our society? What are some things you could do to make an older person's life better?

8. Honesty is an important quality for us to have. Why is it important to be honest even when no one else is looking? Include some situations that test our honesty.

9. If you owned a convenience store and wanted to hire a kid to work at your store, what kinds of qualities would you want your new employee to have? What kind of interview would you conduct before you hired him? What sort of behavior would you expect him to use while he is working in your place of business?

...Expository Prompts

10. Some people think kids watch too much television, too many movies, and play too many computerized games. If the electrical power was turned off for two months, what sort of things could kids do to have fun? Would this be good or bad? Why?

11. If you and three of your friends were shipwrecked alone on a tropical island, what are some things you could do to stay alive until someone rescued you? What type of personal strengths would you have to use to keep your wits about you?

12. Describe what it would be like if kids went to school in the evening instead of during the daytime. How would things be different? Compare going to school at night with going to school during the day.

13. Every family needs a plan of action in case of a fire in your home. What are some important things your family needs to practice for fire safety? What are some things you can do to help your family stay alive?

14. Celebrating holidays in special ways creates great memories. How does your family celebrate a favorite holiday? (or how do you WISH they did!)

15. Houseplants need our care to flourish and stay healthy. If you planted a lovely plant in a pot to sit in the window of your bedroom, how would you take care of it to keep it growing for a long time?

16. Moms and dads are always giving to their children. Sometimes they do without something in order to have the money to buy clothes or toys their children need. What are some things you could do to show your appreciation? Why is showing your appreciation important in your relationship with your parents?

17. Sometimes kids can be cruel. They say or do things that are hurtful to kids who look different than they do. If a new student who was physically different came to your school, what are some things you could do to make her feel welcome?

18. Lots of people have strong fears called phobias. Some people are afraid of spiders and snakes, others are terrified of high places, and still others are afraid of big dogs. What are you afraid of? Why?

CHAPTER EIGHT
Narrative Handout Sheets

The writing menu is a concept that requires teachers to plan writing projects and activities around themes, units, and academic topics of study. This book has tried to lay out the basics of planning and implementing writing menus in your everyday classroom writing workshops. However, a few handout sheets will be helpful as you teach target skills and the basics of the narrative to young writers.

How can kids improve narrative writing?

Telling good stories is an art. Interesting settings, unusual time frames, writer tricks, grabbers, dialogue, exciting problems, and satisfying solutions are telltale signs of excellent writing. These also make narratives much more enjoyable for the reader. In order to make their stories come alive, kids need to be able to recognize and use all of these skills in and throughout their writing.

The handout sheets in this chapter are primarily for narrative writing and have been designed to help students become familiar with tools professional authors use on a regular basis. In particular, the narrative star (Story Star) is a handy reference guide and pattern for writing exceptionally good stories. A simplified version of this star for kindergarten and first-grade students is available in Chapter Ten along with simplified narrative prompts.

Good stories begin with good planning. One technique to improve narrative writing is to practice the planning stage of story writing. Demonstrate how to plan a great story. Model this several times and ask the kids to give their input, as well. Duplicate the story planner sheet on page 84 for your students. The lower half shows an example of a story in the planning stage and can serve as an example. Now ask kids to plan, but not write, several stories on their own, using the narrative star and the story planner as guides. It is a good practice for kids to plan many stories and keep these plans in their writers' notebooks. The more they plan, the better they get at the overall structure of good stories.

When it's finally time to write a story to completion, kids can choose one of the stories they've already planned. After they've written the rough draft and have the basic plot of the story in place, help them embellish their stories with the various writers' tricks outlined for you on pages 80-81. Other handouts on writing grabbers, dialogue, problems, and solutions are available throughout this chapter.

in a barn
on a farm
in a forest
at FAO Schwartz
Statue of Liberty
in the desert
out at sea
in a house
on a river
in the backyard
in a small village
in space
in the jungle
at a hotel
in a toy store
at the zoo
on the subway
at the library
in Mexico
at a restaurant
at a theme park
in Hong Kong
in Scotland
at a county fair
at the White House
in a lush garden
on an airplane
in a town
at an office
in a skyscraper
at a wedding
at a playground
in the park
in the lunchroom
at a family reunion
at the theater
in court
at the police station
at the fire station
in a temple
at a school
in a hot-air balloon
at the supermarket
at the beach
in a graveyard
at the golf course

in Italy
in Heaven
in the basement
at a shopping mall
in a race car
in a pumpkin patch
on an old highway
down in a hole
in the hospital
around a pond
at church
in our classroom
at the dump

Settings For Narratives

in a rain forest
on a train
in Australia
Gulf of Mexico
at a factory
in the bathtub
during a war
in a spaceship
in a castle
in Japan
at a demolition derby
in an ice cream parlor
in a dungeon
in an operating room
inside a computer
at the doctor's office
at a baseball field
in the back of a limousine
at a birthday party
Kennedy Space Center

on a raft
in a boat
at the North Pole
at the Sphinx
in a large city
in a bank vault
at a soccer field
on a basketball court
at a museum
in Europe
on The Great Plains
at the South Pole
in an apartment
in a meadow
in France
in London
inside a shoe
at summer camp
at a circus
at a gas station
in a prison
at K-Mart
inside a mouth
at a skating rink
in an igloo
on an island
on the moon
on a planet
inside a nut
at the swimming pool
in the kitchen
on the Mississippi River
at the end of the rainbow
in the art room
in a box
down the drain
at a dentist's office
at a construction site
on the Equator
in a helicopter
in the Alaskan mountains
at the Great Wall of China
at Stonehenge
in a cave
on an Indian reservation
on an island

Story settings were compiled by Leslie Silver's third-grade, Lakeview Elementary students, Sarasota, Florida.

WRITERS' TRICKS

Name _____ Date _____

grabber or hook - A sentence that is so interesting, shocking, or
    mysterious it captures the reader's attention right away:
    Darcy, T-beau, and the other slaves hadn't eaten in
    three weeks and knew they hadn't long to live.

descriptive language - Words that create a picture in the reader's mind
    of what the author wants the reader to imagine:
    Murphy's shaggy, brown fur was tangled and matted and dripping with
    muddy water.

juicy color word - A specific color name:
    raspberry red, school-bus yellow, turquoise, oyster white, dove gray

strong verb - An active verb that adds special meaning to the sentence:
    The wounded wolf *crawled* across the frozen field and *struggled* his
    way down into the den.

specific emotion word - A word that names exactly what a character feels:
    Annie felt *pity* for the orphaned kitty.

sensory word - A word that helps the reader see, hear, smell, feel
    or taste something described in the story:
    The *spicy* smell of orange marmalade came from Grandma's kitchen.
    The janitor carefully picked up the jagged, sharp pieces of glass.

simile - Words that compare two things using the words *like* or *as:*
    The goalie defended the net like a fighting tiger.
    Paul was as happy as an elephant with a pile of peanuts.

tagged dialogue - Telling what someone says and letting the reader know
    who is speaking by using ***he said*** or ***she said:***
    "The snow is perfect for sledding," Carrie said.
    "I know!" Tiffany said. "I can't wait till school is out so we can go to
    the playground hill."

special tags - Dialogue tags other than "said" that give clues about the mood of
    the person speaking:
    "You're grounded for one week," Jason's mom snapped.
    "Please don't ground me over the weekend," Jason pleaded. "I've got
    tickets to the big basketball game."

WRITERS' TRICKS...PAGE TWO

tagless dialogue - Telling what someone says without tags:

"You're grounded for one week!"

"Please don't ground me over the weekend. I've got tickets to the big basketball game."

flashback - Taking the reader back in time to let him know something that has happened beforehand

plot clues - Giving the reader clues so he can figure out the action of the story

foreshadowing - Hinting about something important that is going to happen later on in the story

surprise ending - Giving the reader an ending that will be a total surprise

metaphor - Comparing two things that don't normally go together to make a special point:

Thomas was a big ox who could move a piano all by himself.

My husband is 24-carat gold.

onomatopoeia - Words that sound like sound effects:

buzz, drip, beep, crunch, rip, sizzle, pop, snap, ripple, rustle

catchy title - A title that creates interest and makes the reader want to read the story to find out what will happen

"show, don't tell" - giving the reader clues through descriptive language instead of stating the obvious:

Coach blew the whistle loudly and motioned for Thad to take the bench.

Thad's knees began to tremble and his face turned ashen white.

idiom - Using a familiar saying to add to the story's tone and mood:

Clem was bound and determined not to be hornswoggled by a guy who was still wet behind the ears.

"A watched pot never boils," reminded Mrs. Fisher. "Just be patient."

transitional phrases or words - Using phrases that naturally move the story to the next sequence or show its relation to the rest of the story:

An hour after Gerry's warning light went on, his engine died.

In the beginning, Karey thought she could set the tent up by herself.

The next step, Alicia realized, would be to put the worm on her hook.

First of all, I didn't have time to do my homework.

FIVE POINT NARRATIVE STAR

Name _____ Date _____

Introduction - The introduction sets up the story by revealing setting, time frame, and main characters. It "hooks" the reader with a grabber.

Setting - The setting is where the story takes place.

Time Frame - The time frame is when the story takes place.

Main Characters - Main characters have names, physical descriptions, and personalities. Of these three, the personality is what makes us "know" and makes us relate to a character. An author reveals a personality through what a character says and does and by giving clues to the reader.

Grabber - The grabber is a sentence that first grabs the reader's attention. Authors have to hook the reader right away at the beginning of a story with a grabber.

Problem - The story problem is the conflict or event that causes tension and creates interest. The problem makes the reader want to continue reading to find out what happens to the main characters and how the problem is solved.

Effect - This point of the narrative star means how the problem affects the main characters. What complications and emotions does the problem cause?

Solution - The solution is the author's answer to the problem. The problem should give enough details to satisfy all of the reader's questions and move the story towards the conclusion and a satisfying ending.

Takeaway - The takeaway ends the story by telling the reader what the main character learned or how his life was changed.

All five points of the narrative star combine to make great stories.

FIVE POINT NARRATIVE STAR

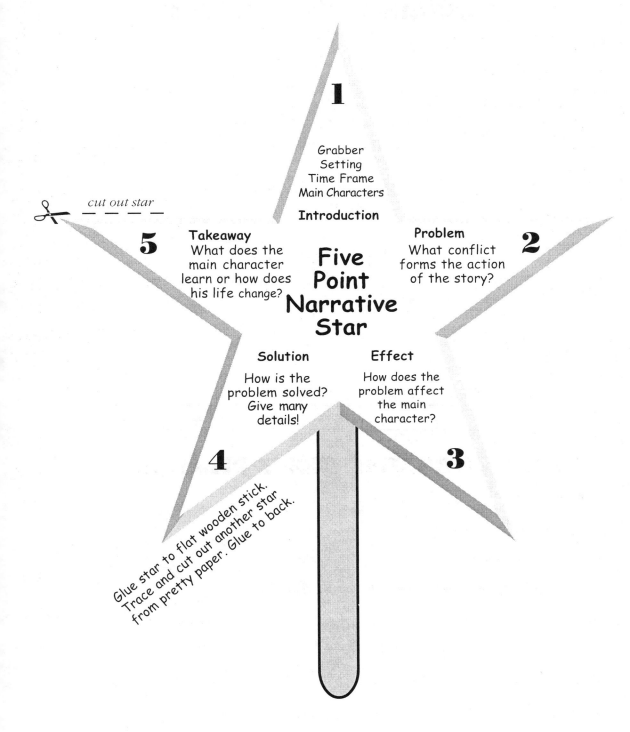

cut out star

1

Grabber
Setting
Time Frame
Main Characters

Introduction

5

Takeaway
What does the
main character
learn or how does
his life change?

**Five
Point
Narrative
Star**

Problem
What conflict
forms the action
of the story?

2

Solution

How is the
problem solved?
Give many
details!

Effect

How does the
problem affect
the main
character?

4

3

Glue star to flat wooden stick.
Trace and cut out another star
from pretty paper. Glue to back.

Cut out the five point narrative star and glue it to a wooden stick.

Now you have an instant reference you can use when you plan a story.

This is only one pattern. There are many ways to tell good stories.

You may choose to glue this star to the back of the star on page 101.

NARRATIVE STORY PLANNER

Introduction:

    Setting:

    Time Frame:

    Main Characters:

Problem:

Effect:

Solution:

Takeaway:

✂ *cut apart*

NARRATIVE STORY PLANNER

---Example---

Introduction

    Setting: My house

    Time Frame: When I was 11 years old

    Main Characters: Me and my grandaddy

Problem: Grandaddy forbids me to touch the riding lawn mower. When he's gone fishing, I try to mow the yard anyway.

Effect: I can't turn off the lawn mower. It keeps going and going. I'm scared!

Solution: I finally have to drive down to the dock to get Grandaddy to turn off the lawn mower. He's mad but he helps me. I apologize. I have to mow the grass for the next four weeks because I disobeyed.

Takeaway: I learn not to disobey Grandaddy.

TAGGED DIALOGUE: OTHER WAYS TO SAY "SHE SAID" OR "HE SAID."

The dialogue tags we use can add hidden meaning and plot clues to our writing. Because authors are supposed to *show* their readers what's going on, instead of *telling* them, one way to give your readers clues is to use special tags instead of the usual "she said, he said."

"I've told you a hundred times not to cook while I'm gone," her mother *scolded*. "You are grounded until next Monday."
"Please don't ground me," Sarah *pleaded*. "We ordered takeout from the Chinese restaurant."

accused	insisted	remarked
admitted	interrupted	repeated
agreed	lectured	reported
announced	mentioned	reprimanded
answered	mumbled	responded
apologized	murmured	retaliated
appealed	muttered	retorted
argued	narrated	revealed
asked	objected	scolded
asserted	observed	shouted
babbled	pleaded	spoke
begged	pointed out	squeaked
bemoaned	pronounced	squealed
bickered	proposed	stammered
blamed	protested	stated
bragged	quarreled	suggested
called	rambled	taunted
cautioned	raved	uttered
charged	reasoned	voiced
chattered	rebuked	whispered
claimed	recited	yelled
commented	refused	yelped
communicated		
confided		
confirmed		
congratulated		
cried		
declared		
denied		
described		
differed		
disagreed		
drawled		
droned		
echoed		
estimated		
exclaimed		
explained		
expressed		
groaned		
guessed		
heckled		
implored		
insinuated		

Kids' Narrative Writing

RUBRIC RACE

★ **6.0** **THE ABSOLUTE WINNER!**
Has all 5 points of the narrative star, awesome details, and uses many creative writers' tricks, including dialogue

★ **5.5** **INDIANAPOLIS 500!**
Has all 5 points of the narrative star, awesome details, and uses several incredible writers' tricks, including dialogue

★ **5.0** **EAT MY DUST!**
Has all 5 points of the narrative star, many details, and several great writers' tricks

★ **4.5** **RACING AND ROARING!**
Has all 5 points of the narrative star, many details, and some good writers' tricks

★ **4.0** **RED HOT COMBUSTION!**
Has all 5 points of the narrative star, many details, and some writers' tricks

3.5 **REVVING YOUR ENGINE**
Has at least 4 points of the narrative star, lots of details and a few writers' tricks

3.0 **RUMBLING LOW**
Has at least 3 points of the narrative star, lots of details and a few writers' tricks

2.5 **NEED A TUNEUP**
Has at least 2 points of the narrative star, some details, and a few or no writers' tricks

2.0 **BACKFIRING**
Has at least 2 points of the narrative star, few details, and no writers' tricks

1.5 **ENGINE TROUBLE**
Has at least 1 point of the narrative star, few or no details, and no writers' tricks

1.0 **OUT OF GAS**
Did write a <u>little</u> on the topic...didn't finish

0 **STUCK IN THE PIT**
Did not try or didn't stay focused

FIND THE GRABBERS

Some beginning sentences can "grab" or "hook" the reader's attention right away. Read the following sentences as if they were each the first sentence of a story. Check the ones that instantly "grab" your attention.

- [ ] Five boys went camping in the woods behind Watson's pond.
- [ ] Greg had never seen a dead body before.
- [ ] I woke to the sound of something dripping on the floor beside my bed.
- [ ] Our teacher, Mrs. Plunkett, is the best teacher at our school.
- [ ] Andy Gilpin would never forget the time a rattlesnake decided to use his sleeping bag for a hiding place.
- [ ] I like going on vacation.
- [ ] The vacation to the beach started out like any other vacation.
- [ ] Hi! My name is Monica and I'm going to tell you about my best friend.
- [ ] If anyone had told Sarah Spooner that she was going to have to jump off a 30-foot cliff, she would never have believed it.
- [ ] The air was running out! We were going to die!
- [ ] Cassandra thought her diary lock was foolproof, but she had a terrible shock coming.
- [ ] Do you have a favorite pet?
- [ ] Sparky, our wonder dog, once saved my life and became a local hero.
- [ ] Christmas is my favorite holiday.
- [ ] It all started on a Saturday afternoon.
- [ ] "I'm too young to die!" I screamed over the raging sound of rushing water.
- [ ] I'll never forget the time Grandmother's girdle came off in church.
- [ ] Terri and Charlene spent the night at my house last Saturday night.
- [ ] "Mom, would you please make octopus cookies?" Stan asked.

REAL LIVE GRABBERS

The following sentences were all written by students to start writing pieces they were working on. Some are good and others are just ordinary. You be the judge! You might get some good ideas for your own stories and writing projects.

1. "Okay," I thought proudly, "This plan is unbeatable."

2. It all started on a dreary, rainy Saturday afternoon.

3. Jingle jangle! Jingle jangle!

4. "Mom, give me just five minutes!"

5. "Ring, ring, ring!"

6. Last week I was going to the living room when I tripped over the skateboard my brother had left in the middle of the floor.

7. It all started on an island off the coast of Florida, an uninhabited island, to be exact.

8. I didn't tell anyone about the time machine.

9. One day a long time ago I had a bad experience.

10. An enormous semi-truck drove down my street faster than a cheetah running through the jungle.

11. One day something extremely eerie happened.

12. Blam! Blam! Gunshots ring out of a forest.

13. I walked around the weird machine.

14. Have you ever heard the expression, "curiosity killed the cat"?

15. Yesterday, when I was watching CNN News, the newscaster said, "Just in! We just heard that on this chilly day a white, snowy creature has escaped from the North Pole."

17. One day Tom Turkey was missing from Farmer Joe's farm.

18. There once was an Indian boy who lived in a hot desert out West.

STORY PROBLEMS

Do you ever wonder what makes a good story "take off"? It's the **problem**. We get to know a few characters and care about them, and then something interesting happens to cause some sort of conflict or problem. This creates tension and interest. As readers, we wonder how the characters will solve the problem. As writers, it's our job to invent problems and ways to solve them. Problems must hold the reader's attention the entire story.

For instance, let's say we're writing a story about an old Indian chief and his grandson. Now we need a problem to make the story "take off." Many things could happen to the chief and boy...

A scorpion burrows into one of their sleeping bags.

The old chief is attacked by a panther and the boy must go for help.

The boy wants to learn to hunt but the other warriors think he is too young.

The boy and his grandfather are separated while they are out scouting.

The chief wants to train the boy at home but some authorities want the boy to go to school in town.

The chief gives the boy a pony of his very own, but it's stolen by another tribe.

They go on a long canoe trip and have to survive a terrible storm.

See how all of these situations present problems? They make us want to read the story to see how it turns out. Problems are interesting to readers. Problems can be funny, scary, adventurous, realistic, fantastic, mysterious, or unusual.

List a few problems that could happen to two best friends who are spending the summer at a lake with their parents and families. Try to come up with ideas that will hold kids' attention throughout an entire story.

_____

_____

_____

_____

Now read one of your best problems to the class. Listen to other kids' ideas. Did you come up with problems that are interesting to read about? Help each other come up with ways to hold the reader's attention. Writers help other writers. That's the way to build a real writing community.

STORY SOLUTIONS

When writers write stories, the problem makes the story "take off" by creating interest. This gets the reader's attention. What satisfies the reader? The solution! The solution is the answer to the problem. Readers want to know how the characters in the story solve the problem or get out of a bad situation. Lots of times kids develop good problems, but then end their stories too quickly without a satisfying solution:

I woke up and it was all a dream.
They all lived happily ever after.
Everything worked out okay after that.

This kind of ending doesn't satisfy the reader! Don't quit writing until you've completely solved the problem. Take your time. Tell what happens. Describe how your characters feel and react. Try to come up with interesting or unusual problem solutions. Don't let your readers figure out everything before you write about it.

Consider this problem: A boy is flying in a two-seater airplane with his Uncle Bob. Suddenly Uncle Bob faints and slumps to the floor. Talk about a problem! There are a number of ways the boy could solve the problem...

1. The boy uses the radio to call for help and the control tower tells him each thing to do in order to land the plane safely.

2. The boy splashes some water on Uncle Bob, who is still too sick to fly the plane. He gives the boy instructions and the boy lands safely.

3. The boy can't reach anyone on the radio and can't wake Uncle Bob. He tries to remember the few things Uncle Bob taught him. The boy takes control and barely manages to land the plane in a semi-crash landing.

4. The boy realizes the plane is going to crash. He radios for help. Since he and Uncle Bob are both wearing parachutes, the boy helps his uncle jump and pulls both their cords. The plane crashes into a mountain but the boy and Uncle Bob land their parachutes in some grass. Mountain rangers rescue them to safety. Uncle Bob is given medical help and the boy receives an award for bravery. He is invited to the White House.

Problems can have lots of different solutions!

CREATING STORY SOLUTIONS

Story problems always create tension or interest. Readers want to know, "How is he going to get out of this?" Story solutions have to satisfy the reader. Come up with some creative solutions for the following story problems:

1. Sylvia and Adrienne are spending a fun Friday evening shopping in the mall. They get so busy trying on clothes at one store that they are accidentally locked in the mall at closing time. All the phones have been shut down!

2. Tom, Danny, and Kareem go canoeing together on the Oonawassee River. A storm is on its way. The boys notice they are surrounded by alligators.

3. Maria borrows her older sister's blouse without asking her permission. While she is wearing the blouse, she accidentally spills mustard on it. When she tries to get the stain out, she rubs a hole in the   material. Her sister needs the blouse for a date that evening.

4. Mrs. More's fourth-grade class goes   on a camping trip. During a scavenger hunt, four kids get separated   from the group and are lost in the woods. Suddenly, they see   a huge grizzly bear!

5. Ashleen wants to be a cosmetologist when she grows up. Already she's been practicing cutting hair on her little sister's dolls. She talks her best friend, Caitlin, into letting her cut her hair. She has trouble getting it even, so she keeps having to cut off a little more and a little more. The hair cut is a disaster!

6. One beautiful day at the beach, Shawn rides the waves in his inflatable, rubber boat. Some minnows swim close and he becomes interested in trying to catch a few with his hands. Before he knows what has happened, he has drifted way too far from shore. As a matter of fact, he can hardly see shore!

7. Wanda and Patty are always being teased by their friends Ryan and Joel. The boys play tricks on the girls and then laugh at them. The two girls decide to teach the guys a lesson.

8. The Royal Tigers baseball team hasn't won a game all season. Their coach has just about given up hope. The boys are depressed about their defeat. Josh decides to do something that will help the team win their upcoming game against the Sand Sharks on Saturday.

9. Karen is home alone one afternoon after school fixing herself a snack in the kitchen. Looking out the window, she notices a creepy looking man coming out of her dad's storage shed. He is taking her new bicycle!

10. Temekah wants to go on the youth trip with her church youth group. The problem is the trip costs $100 and she only has $17. Her best friends, Kiki and LaToya, have already raised their money and are begging Temekah to come, too.

CHAPTER NINE
Expository Handout Sheets

The two basic categories of writing, narrative and expository, go together like two sides of a coin and must permeate the writing menus you plan. Kids should know the meaning of the words narrative and expository and know how to recognize what category a piece of writing falls into. They should also be familiar with both narrative and expository writing prompts and the word clues that tell them which is which. Some handout sheets have been provided in this chapter to help you teach these imporant concepts and to ensure more successful writing menus.

What types of expository writing must kids be familiar with?

Kids should know how to:
present information
explain directions
give an opinion
persuade the reader

From a basic paragraph to a how-to paragraph to a five-paragraph essay, all expository writing enables kids to organize information and support their findings with details and reasons. When planning the writing menu, be sure to include many forms of expository writing from which kids can choose

What basic expository skills do kids need to know?

Students express opinions and talk easily about things they're interested in. After they are able to write several expository sentences on a given subject, it's time to organize the structure of their writing into the basic paragraph. When students master the simple structure of a basic paragraph, they form a foundation for all other amplified expository writing.

Both narrative and expository writing deal with creativity and content. When telling a story, the emphasis is more on creativity. When writing an expository piece, however, the emphasis is more on content: How much information has been recorded? How weighty is this piece? How good of a job did this kid do supporting his opinion or premise?

The Basic Paragraph

Step One: Select a topic

Teachers and students both need to be able to select writing topics.

Children must be able to write from prompts or assigned topics. They will be required to do so in middle school, high school, and college. However, teacher-generated prompts should have genuine purpose and motivate kids to investigate feelings or knowledge. Vapid prompts such as, "What I did over summer vacation," or, "I am a gumball in a gumball machine. Tell about my day," are lame. They have little validity or ability to inspire. The writing menus you plan should provide a smorgasbord of selection and a variety of genres and interests.

It is crucially important to frequently allow young writers to select their own writing topics. Encourage children to investigate subjects that appeal to them. The ability to generate writing topics is a valuable skill and a step toward independent learning. Freedom to choose creates ownership. Be sure to include a section on the writing menu where kids can generate their own topics and projects.

Ask students to write their topics or project titles on sticky notes and to stick them on their desktops. This helps them stay focused. It's also easy for you to see what students are working on during the writing workshop.

Step Two: Create a List of Details

Convince your kids how much they already know by asking them to write a list of details about the topic---anything they can think of. With practice, children become adept at listing copious amounts of details. From their lists they will later generate topic sentences as well as supporting details.

Topic: A Birthday Party

✓ hats	buying a gift	plastic spoons and forks	✓ playing in the back yard
streamers	✓ pin the tail on the donkey	mothers taking pictures	✓ singing Happy Birthday to You
✓ balloons	children laughing	hot dogs	mothers serving kids
✓ cake	✓ presents	✓ kids playing games	someone spilling punch
✓ ice cream	✓ clown	chips	party favors
candles	✓ wrapping paper	paper plates	drop the handkerchief
a big mess	bows	magic show	party clothes

Now ask your writers to select between eight and 15 details that go together. Circle or check them. Each writer's list will be somewhat different from the others. This is the list of details writers will use to write their basic paragraphs.

Step Three: Indent

How do you get kids to remember to indent at the beginning of a paragraph?

If you validate a certain behavior seven times it becomes a lifelong habit. Praise, brag, reward, compliment, set off fireworks, tap dance on top of your desk. Validation is the key to success.

Step Four: Topic Sentence

What rules should you remember when writing a topic sentence?

The topic sentence has the main idea but no details.

Where does the main idea come from?

The main idea comes from the list of details.

What does "main idea" really mean?

The main idea is a big thought about all the details from the list of details.

If kids don't write a list of details in order to come up with a main idea, they tend to write trite topic sentences. For instance, my second graders wrote:

"Taking care of a dog is fun."

"Oh, really?" I countered. "Look at your list of details."

walk him
feed him
give him water
clean his food bowls
brush his fur
give him a bath
take him for a walk

pick up poop from the yard
take him to the vet
play with him lots
pick off ticks and fleas
clip his toenails
comfort him when it thunders
pick up after him

"And you think this kind of activity is FUN?" I asked, mystified.

The kids reconsidered their list.

"No way," they observed, "that's too much hard stuff."

One boy added, "Lots of hard work."

"Responsibility," another kid put in.

Their new topic sentence read, "Taking care of a dog is a big responsibility and lots of hard work."

A main idea with an attitude!

A main idea that reflected truth and depth about the list of details!

A topic sentence has the main idea but NO details.
Kids frequently start paragraphs by putting details in the topic sentence.

On Thanksgiving we eat turkey, pumpkin pie, stuffing, and cranberries.
Mrs. Bennet is my favorite teacher and she has green eyes.
Taking care of a dog is a big responsibility and you have to feed him.

This is a "no no." Topic sentences should be big and broad and talk about the main idea you wish to express, not the smaller details that will fill the middle of the paragraph. A good way to accomplish this is to discourage your writers from using any of the individual details from the list of details in the topic sentence.

Step Five: Underline Topic Sentence

Underlining helps fledgling writers stay focused on the main idea. Underlining the topic sentence also helps a teacher see at a glance what the author considers to be his main idea.

Hidden Treasures

<u>My grandmother has lots of antiques in her attic.</u> There are boxes of old clothes, hats, and shoes. She kept every one of the toys she had as a child and they are worth a lot of money today. I bet she'd be rich if she sold all of them. My great-grandfather's yellow tandem bike is hanging from the rafters. It's more than a hundred years old and two people can ride it at the same time. Grandmother sure has some cool stuff hidden away.

Step Six: Supporting Detail Sentences

Supporting-detail sentences furnish evidence, reasons, and support for the main idea. They establish validity. They give examples, descriptions, and proof. Supporting-detail sentences are the backbone of a paragraph. Kids should try to use every checked detail from their lists of details in their supporting sentences. Several details can be combined to form a single dense sentence. The more details, the better, as long as they go together in harmony.

After a writer has used one of his details, he crosses it off his list. He keeps supporting the main idea with detail sentences until there are no details left. When he has exhausted the checked details, he's ready for the conclusion.

"How long does it have to be?"

"How much do I have to write?"

Kids won't have to ask anymore! Instead of concentrating on the length of a paragraph, emphasize the density of details per sentence. Content: How much has been said? How rich is the information? Some writers go on and on but never really say much. First- and second-grade writers typically include one detail per sentence:

The more supporting details per sentence, the more mature the writing.

My house is pretty.
It is big.
It is white.
I love my house.

As students mature as writers, we can teach sentence combining to help them include more details in a single sentence. Sentence combining produces sentences that are denser and filled with supportive details.

My house is pretty and it is big and white and I love it.

Conjunction overload, to be sure, but at least there are four details in a single sentence. Not bad. The more you tweak it, the more possibilities you'll have. After a lesson on commas, some of the conjunctions disappear.

My house is pretty, big, and white, and I love it.

Eventually, as writers mature, they put the active verb first.

I love my pretty, big, white house.

Sentence combining sets writers up for revision: saying the same information in a better, more concise way. Start your day by writing four or five very short, simple sentences on the board. Then ask students to combine all of the information into one longer sentence. After they have a chance to practice, let students write their newly combined sentences on the board. The results will be lots of interesting ways to combine information in a sentence. Some are hilarious!

Step Seven: Conclusion

The conclusion is usually the weakest part of a paragraph. Conclusions should restate the main idea in a unique, fresh way to summarize the paragraph. Restating reminds readers that what the author thinks is important.

Kids know that restating means saying something again, so when they get to the conclusion, some of them repeat the main idea almost word for word.

Yum Yum!

Breakfast is a good way to start your day. It gives you lots of energy and keeps you from getting hungry. You can have hot foods like scrambled eggs, bacon, toast, and oatmeal. Cold foods like cereal, milk, juice, and doughnuts are good, too. The vitamins these foods have might keep you from getting sick. Families can get together and talk at breakfast. Breakfast is a good way to start your day.

Readers like fresh material. Show students how to start the conclusion a different way. That means not using:

Breakfast is a....

The writer has already used a couple of important words: breakfast, good, start, day. If he can restate the main idea using different words, his conclusion becomes more powerful. He could have used any one of the following:

We should look forward to breakfast every morning.

Mmmmm! Breakfast is delicious!

We'd run out of steam without breakfast.

We feel good all day when we eat a marvelous morning meal.

All four sentences restate the main idea, *breakfast is a good way to start your day,* in a unique way. Each would complete the paragraph by reminding the reader of the most important thought.

The concept of restating is abstract and requires lots of practice to become good at it. Help students practice restating well-known terms and phrases. Guess the answers or invent new ones. Make "practice restating" a writing game.

Step Eight: Underline Conclusion

As kids are learning to write the basic paragraph, ask them to underline their concluding sentences. As they underline, they should check to see if the conclusion restates the main idea in different words. Any wavy or broken line will do so that the conclusion looks different from the topic sentence.

Step Nine: Title

The title should be written after the paragraph is finished. This helps young writers to focus on the main idea instead of the title. A title is not absolutely necessary but it adds a finishing touch to a piece of writing.

Titles should be catchy and interesting so the reader will be enticed to read the paragraph that follows. The more mature the writing, the more intriguing the title. Tell writers not to give away too many clues—to make the reader guess!

Writing a good title is an accomplishment. Kids need help learning this skill. Writing a title can be a little confusing because kids have been taught to write in complete sentences. When it comes to titles, however, we're usually looking for a phrase or sentence fragment. Titles should have five words or less. This keeps younger writers from trying to write a whole sentence or giving away too much information. Putting a title on writing is like adding a lovely bow to a present.

Kids need practice learning to write titles. Read a basic paragraph and ask your students to write as many possible titles as they can come up with on the board. Discuss which ones would grab your attention and which ones are ordinary. Consider the titles of popular, well-known stories and come up with alternative titles. Read newspaper articles aloud and ask kids to write a simple title.

When students finish a piece of writing, ask them to come up with three or four possible titles. During peer conferences, they can poll other kids to see which ones they like best.

Step Ten: Check Your Work

Reading a piece aloud to herself is a great way for a writer to catch her mistakes. The ears catch more errors than the eyes. After your students have written rough drafts, ask them to read them aloud and correct all the errors they find. Then repeat the process. They almost always find more mistakes and can make corrections before asking peers or the teacher to read their papers.

WRITING A BASIC PARAGRAPH

List of Details...The Beach

✓ sand   ✓ seagulls   ✓ shells

✓ shore   ~~towel~~   ✓ tan

✓ swim   ✓ walks   ✓ sun

~~lifeguard~~   ✓ waves   ✓ sandcastle

✓ blue-green   ✓ picnic   ~~rubber raft~~

Beach Bum Day

Going to the beach is a wonderful way to spend a day.
I love to swim in the blue-green waves that crash on the shore.
Sometimes my children and I take long walks and look for shells in
the wet sand. When we tire, we stop and build a sandcastle or feed
the seagulls scraps from our picnic. I always look forward to relaxing
in the sun and trying to get a tan. A trip to the beach is my personal
formula for enjoyment.

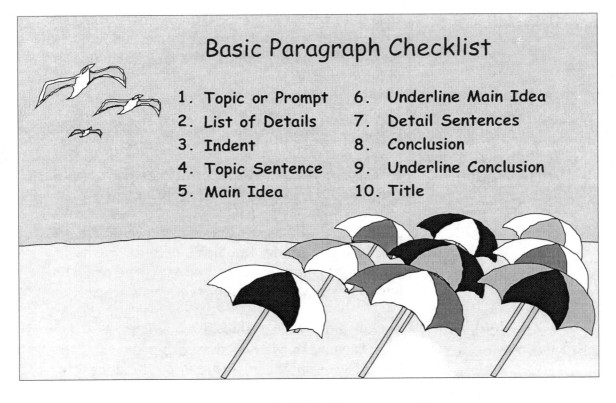

Basic Paragraph Checklist

1. Topic or Prompt
2. List of Details
3. Indent
4. Topic Sentence
5. Main Idea
6. Underline Main Idea
7. Detail Sentences
8. Conclusion
9. Underline Conclusion
10. Title

PRACTICE RESTATING

Restating means to say the same thing in different words. Authors often have to restate to show readers how important their point is. Here are some examples of nouns that have been restated in different words. See if you can come up with some more on your own.

Term	Restated
American flag:	Old Glory, our nation's symbol, stars and stripes, the red, white and blue, America's banner, the symbol of freedom, the star spangled banner, Betsy Ross's home-economics project
Florida:	The Sunshine State, The Peninsula State, Home of the Seminole Indians, America's retirement center, the theme-park capital of America
America:	The United States, the USA, Land of the Free, Home of the Brave, my country, land of my birth, land of liberty, the new world, land of opportunity
graveyard:	the bone yard, the scull orchard, the place people are dying to get into, the final destination, grave, cemetery, Tombstone Town, burial ground
baseball:	America's pastime, Harry Carey's favorite sport, Abner Doubleday's invention, home-run heaven, hurling the old horsehide, the sport that made Babe Ruth famous
mirror:	looking glass, peer glass, reflection, reflector, opposite image
White House:	1600 Pennsylvania Avenue, the President's house, the Oval Office, the first family's home
Santa Clause:	St. Nick, jolly old St. Nicholas, the jolly old elf, Kris Kringle, Santa, Rudolph's master, Father Christmas, the guy in the red suit, the one who knows if you've been naughty or nice
Arnold Schwarzenegger:	Mr. Olympia, Maria Shriver's husband, The Terminator, Conan the Barbarian, an actor, Mr. Schwarzenegger, Arnie Baby, Kindergarten Cop

FIVE-PARAGRAPH EXPOSITORY ESSAY STAR

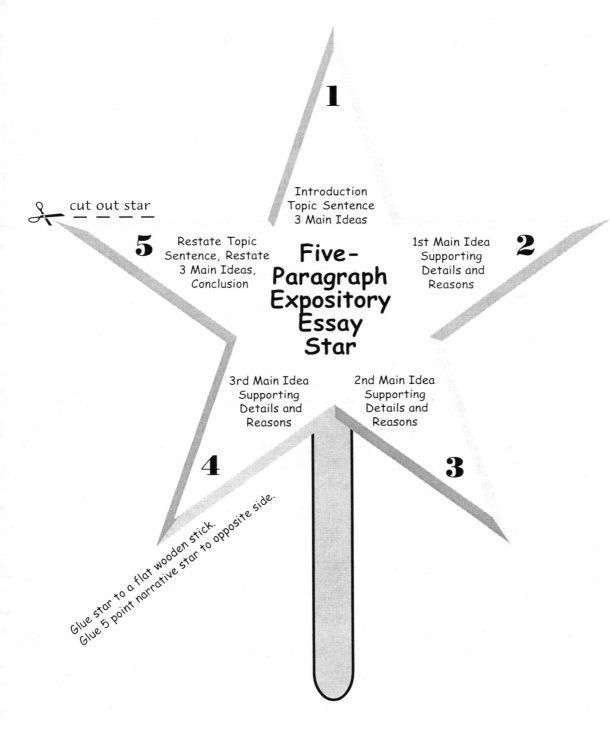

cut out star

1
Introduction
Topic Sentence
3 Main Ideas

Five-Paragraph Expository Essay Star

5
Restate Topic
Sentence, Restate
3 Main Ideas,
Conclusion

2
1st Main Idea
Supporting
Details and
Reasons

3
2nd Main Idea
Supporting
Details and
Reasons

4
3rd Main Idea
Supporting
Details and
Reasons

Glue star to a flat wooden stick.
Glue 5 point narrative star to opposite side.

Cut out the five-paragraph expository essay star. Glue it back-to-back to the five point narrative star. Now you have a handy writing reference pattern. The five-paragraph expository essay is one type of formal writing you will be asked to do in middle school, high school, and college.

Kids' Five-Paragraph Expository Essay
ENDURANCE EVENT

★ **6.0** **THE DETERMINATOR!**
Perfectly written, extremely creative, dazzling and deep

★ **5.5** **CYCLING CYBORG!**
Almost perfect, very creative, unusually insightful and deep

★ **5.0** **LEAN, MEAN, CYCLING MACHINE!**
Has introduction, 3 main ideas, many excellent supporting details,
several good writers' tricks, a conclusion, transitional phrases,
very creative

★ **4.5** **MUSCLE BURNING MANIAC!**
Has introduction, 3 main ideas, many supporting details,
several good writers' tricks, a conclusion, transitions, creative

★ **4.0** **OLYMPIAN!**
Has introduction, 3 main ideas, many supporting details,
several good writers' tricks, transitions, and a conclusion

3.5 **STRUTTING YOUR STUFF...**
Has introduction, at least 3 main ideas, lots of supporting details,
several good writers' tricks, transitions

3.0 **GETTING THERE...**
Has at least 3 main ideas, lots of supporting details and
some writers' tricks

2.5 **NEED TO EAT YOUR WHEATIES...**
Has at least 2 main ideas, some supporting details, and
few or no writers' tricks

2.0 **PUFFING UPHILL...**
Has at least 2 main ideas, few supporting details,
and no writers' tricks

1.5 **BROKEN SPOKE...**
Has at least 1 main idea, few or no details,
and no writers' tricks

1.0 **FLAT TIRE...**
Got started on the topic...didn't finish

0 **TOTAL WRECK...**
Didn't start or didn't stay focused

NARRATIVE AND EXPOSITORY PROMPTS

The word *narrative* means writing that tells a story. Most good stories have a problem or challenge to solve. Stories take place over a period of time. Narratives can be made up, called *fiction*, or true, called *nonfiction*.

The word *expository* means writing that explains. When we explain something we usually list facts or reasons why we believe something is true or important. Writers explain by giving information, giving directions, sharing an opinion, and persuading their readers.

Sometimes authors are asked to write about something. This topic is called the *prompt*. Before you write to a prompt, you must decide whether the prompt asks you to tell a story or to explain something.

Narrative Prompts

A narrative prompt asks you to tell a story:

Imagine you make friends with a dolphin while you are swimming in the ocean. You notice a message tied around its neck. The note reads, "Help! I'm wounded and stranded on a small island about 50 miles due east off the coast of Key West. Please send help!" What happens?

Another narrative prompt might be something that has happened to you:

Everyone has lost or broken something that was valuable or special. Tell about a time you lost something. How did you lose it? How did you feel? Did you get into trouble? What happened? How did the situation end? What did you learn?

Expository Prompts

An expository prompt asks you to explain something:

Taking care of a pet is an important responsibility. Think of some ways in which people take care of pets. Tell why animals depend on people to help them. Explain why it is a rewarding experience to take care of an animal.

Explaining something requires support with reasons and details:

Convince the teacher to take your class on a two week camping trip. Give reasons and convincing arguments why the trip would be a good learning experience.

KNOW YOUR PROMPTS!

Can you tell the difference between a narrative prompt and an expository prompt? Read the list of prompts below. Decide whether you would have to tell a story or explain something. Write N in the blank if the prompt is narrative. Write E in the blank if the prompt is expository.

_____ Explain why having good friends is important.

_____ Why do we have to take care of our teeth?

_____ Tell about the time you skipped school and got caught.

_____ Convince the class to vote for your best friend for class president.

_____ Write a story about a boy who becomes the youngest professional basketball player in America.

_____ Tell about two girls who accidentally set the kitchen on fire while they are making doughnuts.

_____ Which restaurant is your favorite, and why?

_____ Explain why a tiger would not make a good pet.

_____ All American citizens should vote. Do you agree or disagree? Why?

_____ Teachers should not give homework over the weekend.

_____ Make up a story about a kid who becomes a cowboy for a summer.

_____ Which holiday is your favorite, and why?

_____ America is the greatest country in the world.

_____ Write a story about two girls who get to meet a famous person.

_____ Pretend you have been asked to be in a famous Hollywood movie. What happens?

_____ Kids should wear uniforms to school.

_____ Tell about the time you were attacked by a fierce tiger in the jungles of India. Give lots of details in your story.

_____ Elementary kids should be allowed to participate in the Olympics.

_____ Fishing is more fun than playing video games.

CHAPTER TEN

Special Helps for Little Writers

What a privilege it is to teach kindergarten and first-grade children the joys of oral and written self-expression and communication. Little children come to us as pliable and moldable as sculpting clay. Usually they are imaginative and lack inhibitions, exploring their new world of formal education like an adventurous scientist on an expedition: searching, examining, experimenting, discovering, and reacting. If you can foster a love for writing at this stage, the battle is won. Writing becomes a natural, daily part of the curriculum.

Oral Communication

Most kindergarten and first-grade students are great oral writers, sharing stories, experiences, opinions, information, big lies, and family secrets. Verbal language is the main way they communicate with others. They already "write out loud," both verbally and spontaneously, that which we will teach them to record on paper. Oral language comes about naturally and is full of rich description.

A few kids have to be coaxed out of their shyness, and this is done with lots of encouragement and validation. One-on-one conversations are great starting points. Gradually work these children into partnerships, small group discussions, and entire classroom share sessions. Shy kids who would die a thousand deaths if they had to "perform" in front of a live audience sometimes open up in front of the VCR camera, tape recorder, or small group.

Bonding activities are crucial to kindergarten and first-grade classes as they foster the type of environment in which writers thrive. Teach young writers the basic etiquette of a safe, non-threatening writing community:

Be a good listener.
Compliment others.
Never make fun of someone else.
Allow different opinions.
Help fellow writers.

The games and handouts in this chapter have been designed to help teach writing to fledgling, primary-grade writers. Many involve oral writing skills.

The Story Star

Name _____

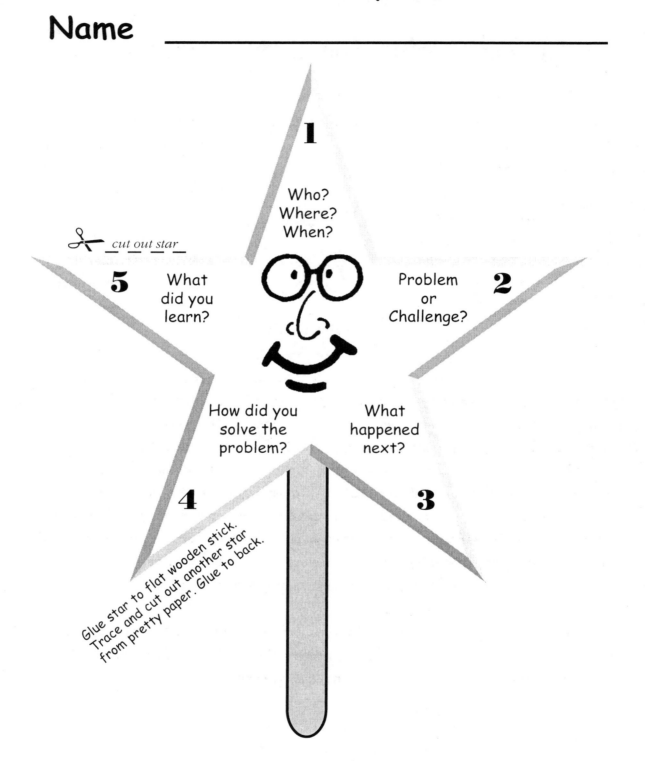

1 Who? Where? When?

2 Problem or Challenge?

3 What happened next?

4 How did you solve the problem?

5 What did you learn?

✂ cut out star

Glue star to flat wooden stick. Trace and cut out another star from pretty paper. Glue to back.

Cut out the five point narrative star and glue it to a wooden stick. You can use the star when you plan and write a story. There are many ways to write good stories. The story star is one good way.

ORAL WRITING GAMES FOR EMERGENT WRITERS

I am the farmer - Select someone to be the farmer. All the rest of the kids pretend they are farm animals — chickens, ducks, geese, horses, mules, pigs, goats, cats, dogs, etc. Tell the class that for years the animals have lived with the farmer but have never been able to tell him anything. Of course, it is because they are unable to speak. On one special night, at the stroke of midnight, the farm animals get to talk, just like people. The farmer goes around to each individual animal and says, "I am the farmer. Who are you and what would you like to say?" Every animal tells the farmer his name and thinks up something to say.

Examples:

"I am the pig. I would really like a swimming pool to swim in after I've been in the stinky, gooey mud all day."

"I am the horse. Please don't ride me again until you go on a diet."

"I am the goose. I'd like some more grain and some fresh straw for my bed."

I'd like you to know - Give children pictures of a variety of working and professional people. Each child looks at a picture for a few minutes and thinks of things to tell the class about the job that is pictured. One at a time, each comes to the front, holds up a picture, and says, "I'm a _____ and I'd like you to know _____."

Examples:

"I'm a mechanic and I'd like you to know that I work on motors."

"I'm a secretary and I'd like you to know I have my own desk."

"I'm a fireman and I'd like you to know that I drive a firetruck. I also help people who have been in car wrecks."

How Will You get there? - Show a poster or pictures of many different types of transportation. Show maps or posters that picture many different places in the world. Each child thinks of a place she'd like to go and a method of transportation to get there. When called on, she says, "I'm going to _____."
The teacher asks,
"How will you get there?" and the child answers,
"I'm going by _____ so _____."
The child tells what type of transportation she will use then adds a bit more information to make her answer interesting.

...MORE ORAL WRITING GAMES

Examples:

"I'm going to Disney World. I'm going by boat so I will be able to see big, scary, sharks swimming in the ocean."

"I'm going to Montana. I'm going by helicopter so I can look out the window and see buffalo grazing down below on the plains."

Would you describe it, please? - Divide the class into two groups, the "questions" and the "answers." The object of the game is to get kids to use descriptive language. The first "question" person asks, "Would you describe a _____, please?" The first "answer" person responds, "A _____ is _____."

Examples:

Q - "Would you describe a dinosaur, please?"

A - "A dinosaur is rough, scaly, enormous, brown, and has huge teeth."

Q - "Would you describe an octopus, please?"

A - "An octopus is gray, has two eyes, and has eight legs with suckers on them."

What could happen? - List several characters or show a magazine picture of several people. Then create a short scenario about the characters. Next, ask the class, "What could happen?" A simple scenario might be: *Two cousins sleep all night in a tent in the back yard.* Allow kids time to think before they present answers, perhaps over night. Listen to as many responses as time allows and encourage discussion. Kids may ask each other questions to stimulate those creative juices.

Examples:

"A tiger crawls in the cousins' tent and they have to escape before it catches them."

"They accidentally set the tent on fire."

"A big bug flies in the tent and bites one of them on the nose."

"They hear a spooky noise and run for the house."

The ice cream store - Pretend to be the owner of an ice cream store. Ask several kids to act like they are coming to the store to buy ice cream. They line up to the side, awaiting their turns. The rest of the class sits in front like an audience. One by one, as the buyers enter the store, the owner greets them by a fictitious name, asks what they'd like to buy, and then engages them in

impromptu, fictitious conversations. The buyers must respond with realistic answers and stay in character. Later, the audience can discuss who sounded natural and convincing and how to write realistic dialogue for characters.

...MORE ORAL WRITING GAMES

Examples:

T - "Why, hello, Mrs. Wiggins. And what would you like to buy this afternoon?"

C - "I think I'll have a double scoop of chocolate, thank you."

T - "Where are your children this fine afternoon? You usually have them with you."

C - "Shorty's playing softball, and the twins are visiting their auntie."

T - "What time are you picking them up?"

C - "Right after the game."

It's Rhyme Time - This game makes use of rhyming couplets and is a great way to introduce poetry. Recite one-and-a-half lines of a couplet and let the children think of possible endings that complete the rhyme.

Examples:

"I looked in my pocket and found a frog, He jumped right out and _____."
(sat on a dog, bumped into a hog, fell on a log, started to jog)

"I went up the hill to see Miss Sue, But the only one home was _____."
(Little Boy Blue, Karen and you, a cat eating glue, a man without a shoe)

You wouldn't believe - Start the game by saying, "You wouldn't believe the time I _____," and finish the statement in one sentence. Try to make your statement funny, shocking, or scary. Kids follow suit, going around the circle until everyone has had a turn.

Examples:

"You wouldn't believe the time I got stuck in an elevator."
(got a fish bone caught in my throat, saw my cat having kittens, hit a home run, ate an ant on my watermelon, had my tonsils taken out, caught two crabs in a net)

True or false? - Everyone thinks of something he has really done. He also makes up something that never happened. He shares the two facts with the group. The group tries to guess which fact is really true. Each kid wants to stump the class!

Examples:

"I saw a baby wolf in my backyard." (false)

"I found a starfish at the beach." (true)

Which statement is true?

"I have an albino frog in my aquarium at home." (true)

"One time I went water skiing and sat on my dad's shoulders while he skied." (false)

Kids hold up paper plates that say TRUE and FALSE to cast their votes. For every person who votes for the FALSE statement the author gets one point.

...MORE ORAL WRITING GAMES

For your information - Divide the class into two teams, A and B. Team A thinks up common nouns. Team B lines up in front of Team A so they are face to face, a few feet apart. The first "A" says his noun (ketchup, whale, key, etc.), and the first "B" must say, "For your information, _____," and list as many details about the noun as he can think of. He has 30 seconds to answer and his team gets one point for every fact he lists. After 30 seconds it's the next pair's turn.

Examples:

A - "A kite."

B - "For your information kites are made out of paper, they fly in the sky, each has a string, each has a long tail, they have bright colors on them." (5 points)

In my opinion - The teacher, or "It," starts the game by asking, "What kind of fruit is the very best?" or "Who is the coolest person on TV?" or "What's a really fun thing to do on a Saturday afternoon?" Kids think for a few minutes until they have ready answers. They respond by saying, "In my opinion, _____."

Please, Can we go? - This oral writing game stresses the importance of WHO? WHAT? WHEN? WHERE? WHY? and HOW? The object of the game is for kids to persuade the teacher to take the class to a certain place or event. Just saying "Please!" isn't enough. Kids have to convince the teacher they should go by giving all the important information about the trip. This is a fun game to play in teams, with each member of a team answering one of the key questions about the trip. Word cards are helpful reminders of the questions.

examples:

C - "Please, can we go to the beach?"

T - "You'll have to convince me."

C - "We all want to go. Sarah's parents have agreed to be our chaperones."

C - "We will need to take towels and bring our swimsuits."

C - "We could go on Saturday when there is no class."

C - "Let's go to Coquina Beach. It's the closest and nicest beach."

C - "Going to the beach is a great way to have fun. You could relax in the sun."

C - "We could take the big bus we use for field trips. My daddy would drive for us."

C - "Our class could gather shells for the science table."

C - "We can pack picnic lunches and eat together and share."

WRITING PROMPTS
FOR LITTLE FOLKS

1. Who is your favorite family member? What makes this person so special? What kinds of things do the two of you do together?

2. What are some things boys and girls can do to keep their bedrooms clean? Why is your bedroom important to you?

3. What kind of pet would you like to own? What are some things you'd do to take care of your pet?

4. If you had a camera and could take a picture of anyone in the whole world, who would it be? Why do you think this person is so special?

5. Being a mommy or a daddy is hard work. What are some things mommies and daddies do for their children?

6. Many people in our school work hard to make it a nice place for children. Who is one person who works hard, and what does he do?

7. Some people are afraid of the dark. What is one thing you are afraid of? Write about it and draw a picture.

8. You've learned many things at school this year. What is the favorite thing you've learned? Why is it your favorite?

9. Some kids are bullies at school and on the playground. Have you ever seen a bully? What did he do? How did he act? Why is being a bully wrong?

10. Not everyone looks the same. Some people have different color hair and eyes that are shaped differently. Would you still be friends with a person who looks different? Why?

11. Many interesting creatures live in the ocean. Describe a sea creature and tell some things you know about it.

12. Do you think it is important to be honest? What are some ways you can show others you are an honest person? Tell about a time someone hurt your feelings by being dishonest.

13. How do you get ready for school in the morning? Write about some of the things you do each morning.

14. Why is it important to be friendly to all the kids in your class? How would someone feel if other children wouldn't play with him?

15. Exercise is important for a healthy body. What are some ways you can get exercise every day to stay healthy?

16. Everyone likes to feel proud. What is something you've done to make yourself or others feel proud?

17. Pretend you are the principal of your school. Tell about what happens during your day.

18. Write a story about a little dog who lives at the pet store. He wants to be adopted. What happens?

19. Pretend you find a strange box on the way home from school. Something inside is glowing with light. What's in the box? What happens next?

20. Tell about a time when you got hurt. What happened? Who helped you? How did you get better?

21. Make up a story about something very silly that happens at school. Make your story funny!

22. Helpers are kind. Tell about a time when you were a big help to someone. What problem did you help with? How did helping make you feel? What did the other person say when you finished?

23. Pretend you are going to perform with the circus. What type of act will you do? What happens? How do you feel when you are in front of all the children? Tell some of the things the other circus performers say to you in your story.

24. Many kids think they would like to have lots of money. What would you do if you had lots of money?

25. Write a story about two friends who find a paper bag full of jewelry on the sidewalk. How do they find it? Who owns the jewelry and how did it end up on the sidewalk? What do the kids do with the jewelry? How do they feel?

26. Grandparents are special people. Write a true story or make one up about an adventure you've shared with one of your grandparents.

27. Tell about the first day you came to school. What happened? How did you feel? Write about the people you met and the things you did.

28. Pretend you live long ago in the West during the time of the cowboys. Write a story about having to go to school on horseback. What adventures happen? Make your story exciting!

29. Imagine you wake up one morning and find a packet of magic beans on your window sill. Write a story about planting the magic beans. See if you can come up with a wild adventure.

30. If you were walking by yourself and a stranger stopped his car to talk to you, what things would you do to make sure you would be safe from harm?

CHAPTER ELEVEN

Guided, Layered Revision

As kids are working on various projects for the writing menu, they will need to read and revise their writing several times. Too often children are in the habit of writing a rough draft then announcing, "I'm done." When it comes to revision, kids usually don't have a clue how to improve their writing. They can't seem to see weaknesses or mistakes that are glaringly obvious to someone else.

Guided revision is one way to help children improve their writing. The teacher guides revision, targets one skill at a time, and gives suggestions for improvement. These revision sessions are done in layers, or short time periods.

A few tips will help your students with revision:

✓ Write rough drafts in pencil.
✓ Skip lines when writing rough drafts by writing on computer paper with alternating lines of green and white stripes (greenbar paper).
✓ Revise in colored ink, using a new color for each revision layer.
✓ Ask students to add new material in the spaces above or below the line.
✓ Never call a rough draft a "sloppy copy."

During the first 15 minutes of the writing workshop, target one or two specific skills to highlight for revision. Using the chalkboard or the overhead projector, model the skills you're looking for, then ask the class to apply them to a story or piece they are working on. Consult the grade-appropriate target skills list (Chapter Three) for ideas. Show lots of sample writing and good examples.

When students write in pencil, revising in colored ink gives the teacher an instant visual clue as to how many times a student has added to or changed his writing. Each session you guide adds another layer of revision, reflected by a different color of ink. Kids are also free to revise on their own and use yet another color. When the teacher guides revision in several sessions, kids are trained how to improve writing and add embellishments in several "layers." They love using different colors of ink and take pride in the creative process.

It's important to foster the idea of improving what has already been written. If something is worth writing, it's worth improving. Writing must go through several transformations before publishing. Soon students get used to the idea of revising four, five, or six times before a rough draft is ready for publication.

How can kids make short, immature sentences better?

One of the first steps in teaching guided, layered revision is to help students amplify writing. Put a simple, short sentence on the board. Ask kids to copy the sentence on their own greenbar paper. Hold up a sign that has either WHO, WHAT, WHEN, WHERE, WHY, or HOW printed on it.

Instruct students to include that specific information in the simple sentence, making it more informative and descriptive. They can use proofreaders' arrows to point to their additions in the margins or add the information to the beginning, middle, or ending of the sentence. Hold up two or three more signs that specify additional information. You can ask for a juicy color word, strong verb, descriptive word, etc. Compare final sentences or let kids write their amplified sentences on the board. The more they practice this type of exercise, the better they become at being able to revise and amplify short, immature sentences in their own writing.

☹ Example: **It rained.**

☺ Revision:
When   Where   Who
Last night on our way home from the ballgame, we got

Strong Verb   Descriptive Word
drenched in the pouring rain.

Here are some examples of simple sentences you might target for improvement:

1. The dog bit me.
2. Mom cooked breakfast.
3. Nancy fell down.
4. The birds built a nest.
5. We went fishing.
6. My daddy is sick.
7. I love spaghetti!
8. The boy is hiding.
9. Our visitors are late.
10. I had a party.
11. The shell is pretty.
12. Mr. Brown needs a job.
13. I have to rake the yard.
14. The flowers are blooming.
15. The truck raced by.
16. Farmer John plowed his fields.
17. The sky is cloudy.
18. Hiking is fun.
19. Ice cream sodas are good.
20. I bought a cat.
21. He has sand in his shoes.
22. I'm going on vacation.
23. The old woman screamed.
24. Stan pinched his sister.
25. The stars shine.
26. Judy got in trouble.
27. The hamburger was big.
28. Science is interesting.

Use signs to target specific information for guided, layered revision.

Who? Where?
What ? Why?
When? How?

✂

Print WHO, WHAT, WHEN, WHERE, WHY or HOW here.

Glue shield to cardboard, laminate for guided, layered revision.

Revision

Name _____   Date _____

The Best Day

Saturday is my favorite day of the week. You

can do lots of stuff on Saturdays. I always sleep

late. My mom cooks a good breakfast. I like to watch

cartoons for a while. My best friend and I go play

outside. Sometimes we go fishing. Once in a while my

family goes to the movies. Saturdays are cool.

Revising means making big changes, describing, or adding bits of information. Revising makes our writing better and more interesting for the reader.

Read the paragraph above. Most of the sentences are short. They need descriptive words and more details. Ask yourself who? what? when? where? why? and how? as you read each sentence. Draw a caret or arrow to the white space above each line and and add your revisions there.

What other areas are prime targets for revision?

Specific vocabulary.

When children reach eight or nine, begin pointing out that while some words give us a general idea of meaning, other words are better because their meaning is clear and precise.

Compare:	To:
I had a bad day.	**I felt humiliated in front of the whole team when I dropped the ball.**
Steak is good.	**Steak tastes delicious.**
Suzy's a creep.	**I get angry when Suzy copies my ideas.**

The first set of sentences tell us general information. They leave questions in our minds. The second set of sentences is very specific. We know exactly what the writer meant to convey. They are clear, precise, and informative.

Developing writers often use words that connote positive or negative degrees. Words such as *good, great, awful* or *bad* are degree words. They are standard, usable words; some are even advanced vocabulary words. However, they are not specific in meaning. They can have more than one meaning:

I feel *great* today.
The brownies you baked are *great!*
Hey! You smell *great.*
It would be *great* if you could give me
    a ride home.
Would you do me a *great* favor?
I think it's *great* that Coach Paul is
    being honored by the team.
Who is that *great* looking new guy?
Oh *great!* Another bill to pay.

I feel *bad* today.
Too *bad* you can't go.
Tammy has a *bad* attitude.
Davon got a *bad* grade on his
    report card.
He is one *bad* dude.
I feel *bad* that I said some
    bad things about Marsha.
Sharks are *bad* fish.
This sandwich tastes *bad.*

Each of the uses above means something slightly different. All are usable, but none are specific. Specific vocabulary, or diction, gives writing clarity and lets the reader know exactly what the writer means.

How can I help children avoid using too many degree words?

Brainstorm with your class and make a degree word chart, such as the one below. Write as many positive and negative degree words as your students can think of. Now copy the words onto paper plates, using black marker. Pick a central point, such as the classroom clock, and line up the positive words towards the right, near the ceiling. Line up the negative words towards the left. Remind your students that while these are good words, authors can sometimes substitute better, more specific words.

Negative DEGREE Words

fair
poor
not so good
unpleasant
bad
worse
awful
lousy
horrible
terrible
horrid
dreadful
horrendous

Positive DEGREE Words

fine
pretty good
good
better
great
super
fantastic
terrific
awesome
wonderful
marvelous
extraordinary
stupendous

⬅️

(horrible) (terrible) (awful) (bad) (good) (great) (super) (terrific)

➡️

What can students substitute for degree words?

Specific vocabulary.

During your writing workshop, ask students to take out a recent narrative or information piece and highlight all the degree words with a yellow highlighter. They can refer to the paper plate display, the degree word charts, or lists of degree words in their writer's notebooks.

Next, ask if they could substitute specific words that would show more precise meanings. For example, if a kid has written

Jeremiah felt bad.

he would highlight the word *bad* and try to substitute a specific word and add some additional information:

Jeremiah felt lonely when Carlos stayed gone so long.

The new word greatly improves the maturity and clarity of the sentence and lends itself to amplification of information.

Where can students find lists of specific vocabulary words?

Now encourage your writers to make charts of specific words. Hang long sheets of brown paper or butcher paper from the ceiling down to the floor and put a border around the edges. Hang a pen or marker at each chart and ask your students to add to these charts as they come across words in books, stories, conversations, and writing.

Specific word choice is a vital part of all facets of writing. Take our five senses, for instance. When describing a particular taste, the typical kid might write, "The sandwich tasted yucky," or "Cookies are good." The more specific word might be "The sandwich tasted stale," or "Cookies are delicious."

Brainstorm specific sensory words with students, making charts to go with each sense. Validate students who use specific sensory words in their writing.

66 Mature writing is characterized by specific vocabulary. 99

SENSORY WORDS

TOUCH	SMELL	SOUND	TASTE	SIGHT
rough	smoky	crashing	sweet	round
slippery	buttery	banging	sour	tall
bumpy	dusty	booming	tangy	rumpled
velvety	mildewy	clinking	tart	crumpled
scratchy	fresh	whizzing	spicy	thick
hard	new	popping	fresh	bent
padded	musty	plopping	stale	twisted
melted	musky	dripping	peppery	curved
limp	dank	screeching	burnt	sharp
rigid	spicy	howling	moldy	square
grooved	burnt	bawling	salty	plush
fuzzy	acrid	meowing	oily	puffy
wet	earthy	snapping	creamy	dark
slick	fruity	woofing	acid	long
metallic	flowery	jingling	garlicy	open
cracked	chocolaty	tapping	delicious	dotted
flimsy	leathery	clicking	scrumptious	striped
silky	sweet	splashing	succulent	puckered
gooey	vinegary	slurping	refreshing	new
moist	pungent	whistling	thirst-	ancient
plush	lemony	rustling	quenching	wrinkled
prickly	sharp	crackling	fishy	short
sharp	strong	loud	buttery	bright
curved	cheesy	soft	mouth-	multicolored
hairy	yeasty	muted	watering	see-through
dimpled	old	clanging	fruity	spangled
pointed	rank	roaring	minty	glittery
glassy	rotten	growling	starchy	translucent
oily	decayed	yowling	sweet & sour	opaque
dewy	spoiled	sniffling	juicy	glassy
sandy	perfumey	snorting	meaty	transparent
nubby	woodsy	scratching	hearty	chaotic
steamy	grassy	whispering	smoked	orderly

SPECIFIC EMOTION WORDS

POSITIVE EMOTIONS: "I can feel..."

peaceful	joyful	worthy
relieved	proud	relaxed
excited	calm	encouraged
loyal	free	noticed
safe	loved	pleased
focused	ready	capable
happy	lovable	confident
glad	friendly	cherished
wanted	satisfied	prepared
needed	powerful	attractive
valued	capable	supported
helpful	talented	comfortable
appreciated	accepted	complimented
respected	validated	acknowledged
included	rewarded	independent

NEGATIVE EMOTIONS   "I can feel..."

	dumb	overwhelmed
	mocked	dejected
	hopeless	dissatisfied
	judged	unloved
sad	bored	grouchy
lost	ignored	bossed
ugly	bitter	rejected
weak	embarrassed	bothered
angry	overlooked	disheartened
forced	heartbroken	agitated
fearful	distrustful	interrupted
irritated	stressed	helpless
excluded	criticized	uninformed
guilty	insulted	ashamed
nervous	confused	unprepared
betrayed	ridiculed	disappointed
worried	patronized	frustrated
anxious	discouraged	unappreciated
humiliated		

Name _____ Date _____

Know Your Emotion Words!

Good authors use specific emotion words to let the reader know exactly how a character feels. Using your imagination, complete the following sentences.

1. Carmen felt desperate when she _____.

2. After the game was over, Zeke felt_____,
   because the coach _____.

3. When I saw my grandmother for the first time in two years, I felt _____
   and _____ because _____.

4. The tiny kitten felt _____ when the fireman rescued it from
   high up in the tree.

5. It's always embarrassing to me when _____.

6. Don't ever _____ because it makes me feel _____.

7. Eddie wasn't able to _____ because he felt_____.

8. When I _____, it makes me feel proud and _____.

9. When I think of the victims of the Holocaust, I feel _____ and
   _____ because _____.

10. Sondra showed that she felt_____ and _____ by
    _____.

11. I feel _____ and _____ when my mother makes
    me _____.

12. The absolute best thing that could happen today is _____
    because I would feel _____ and _____.

JUICY COLOR WORDS

See how many color families and individual colors your students can come up with!

RED

ruby
rose
blush
strawberry
cherry
cranberry
rouge
pink
garnet
Christmas
blood
oxblood
rust
barn
fire engine
candy apple
poppy
paprika
magenta
cerise
flaming
sunburn
tomato
fuchsia
scarlet
cinnamon
crimson
carmine

BLUE

baby
sky
navy
midnight
cobalt
royal
country
Wedgewood
denim
powder
robin's egg
azure
periwinkle
steel
slate
ocean blue
aquamarine
cornflower
turquoise
cerulean
sapphire

YELLOW

butter
school bus
egg yolk
marigold
gold
sunflower
cornsilk
banana
lemon

GREEN

lime
fern
olive
drab
army
khaki
seafoam
mint
teal
chartreuse
pistachio
seagreen
pea
forest
lawn
grass

ORANGE

goldenrod
sunset
fluorescent
dayglow
mango
tangerine
pumpkin
persimmon
fiery
coral
peach
saffron

PURPLE

hyacinth
orchid
lilac
lavender
burgundy
periwinkle
violet
bruise
plum
eggplant
aubergine
grape

BROWN

tan
chocolate
cocoa
mahogany
maple
sandy
sienna
moccasin
pecan
walnut
beige
earthen
saddlebrown
terra-cotta
chestnut
bronze

BLACK

jet
ebony
midnight
licorice
pitch
onyx
raven
coal
inky
soot
ebon

WHITE

creme
eggshell
almond
ecru
manila
vanilla
oyster
alabaster
snowy
milky
chalky
bleached
frosted
ivory

GEMS

diamond
ruby
topaz
peridot
emerald
quartz
opal
garnet
citrine

METALLICS

gold
silver
bronze
pewter
steel
platinum
chrome

CHAPTER TWELVE

At The Close
of the Writing Menu Period

After the writing menu period has ended, many facets will need to come together to ensure individual student's success and facilitate the teacher's evaluation of student writing. With good classroom management and pre-planning, the whole process can run smoothly and, ultimately, enhance classroom learning.

What can teachers do in advance to make sure students are prepared for the due date?

At the beginning of the writing menu period, post the due date (or due dates), give it out in writing, and inform parents, as well. If you spread out the due dates over several days, you won't have everyone's work coming in on the same day. That can be a little overwhelming.

As you circulate throughout the room during the writers' workshop during the previous weeks, you will familiarize yourself with each child's progress. Encourage him to complete the work he has contracted for (pages 38-39) as well as a **Writing Menu Point Sheet**. It will be tempting to nag, but try to avoid that trap. Keep validating progress and reminding the class of the many interesting presentations they will have to look forward to at the end of the writing menu due date.

You must tell students in advance whether their projects should be turned in as **rough drafts** (my preference), or recopied, **published works**.

When and how do kids prepare their body of work for evaluation?

At least one week prior to the due date, young authors need to ask several other students to read and respond to their various pieces of writing through **peer conferencing**. Actually, this can be done throughout the weeks of the writing menu period as well as at home. They may also share their works-in-progress in the **Author's chair** for several peers at once.

Another technique that saves extra work at evaluation time is having kids report to one of several **student editors**, students specially trained to look for such details as name on paper, date, papers numbered and in order, title of five words or less, skipped lines, etc. An editor can check off a checklist and "pass" an author with a special stamp or hole-punch, or ask that he make a few corrections.

Students should begin getting their projects in their final form for evaluation at least several days before the due date. This means putting on the final touches, adding pictures, illustrations, charts, maps, etc., editing for spelling, grammar, and conventions (if you've asked them to do so), recopying or publishing their rough drafts (if their writing is unreadable).

How do students turn in their projects?

It is especially nice if students present their projects in a legible condition, in order, and in a folder. Accompanying the folder should be their completed **Writing Menu Point Sheet**. Ideally, all work should be turned in by the prescribed due date, but in an imperfect world, you will need to establish some sort of late work policy that works for your class but is somewhat flexible.

How does the class benefit and gain knowledge from these writing projects?

At the end of the writing menu period, you will schedule a day or several days of presentations. This is a wonderful time when the entire class can learn from and celebrate each other's hard work. By showing, telling about, or presenting one of her projects, each child will have a chance to contribute important information and knowledge to the rest of the class. By doing so, she will also earn extra points that can be added to her evaluation point sheet.

How are writing projects to be evaluated?

By this time, the teacher has spent quite a bit of time creating the writing menu, as well as implementing it and guiding students through layers of revision. Kids have spent several weeks researching, writing, and enhancing their projects. At the close of the writing menu period, you will now evaluate each child's body of work. In particular, you will be looking for **content** and **creativity**. How much has been said? How creatively has this information been presented to the reader?

Spend some time reading and assessing each child's writing projects. Review a child's entire body of work in a **general** sort of way, looking at the whole instead of details. Using the contract and the Writing Menu Point Sheet the student has already filled out, assign points to each of his projects according to

how well he followed directions
how much information he has included in his project
target skills he has used correctly
specific vocabulary word usage
completion
preparation (proper format)
creativity
enhancements
presentation to the class

Next, select one major narrative or expository piece to evaluate more closely. You can assess the piece yourself or you might choose to participate in holistic evaluation with a team of other teachers. At any rate, note content, creativity, and progress, and record comments and suggestions.

Should teachers conference with students?

Absolutely.

Every author craves validation. Every author needs objective suggestions for improving his work. Every author loves to hear what the reader enjoyed about his piece. The teacher/student conference is an indispensable part of the evaluation process. This one-on-one time is a vital step in helping kids improve writing.

First of all, go over the general body of work with each author. Discuss the points that were assigned, points taken away, and bonus points. Involve the author in a discussion of his growth as a writer and progress in his work. Elicit his opinions and viewpoint. Show a sincere appreciation for his efforts and contribution to the class's knowledge pool. Thank him for being part of the class writing community.

How can parents help in the evaluation process?

Encourage all parents to stop by the classroom to see the variety of writing projects produced by your students. Parents get a broader perspective of their own child's progress when they see an assortment of writing samples produced by all students in a given class. Invite them to validate their child's progress as an author and knowledge contributor. Parent involvement speaks volumes to young writers and underscores the importance of writing in your classroom.

Explosive Encouragement for Writers!

I'm impressed.
You are so talented.
You write like magic!

You scared me to death!
This piece touched me.
I've felt the same way.

You are such a gifted author.
Doesn't this make you proud?
This should be in a museum.

Where did you learn words like these?
This reminds me of something that happened to me.
I can't wait to share this with the rest of the class.
You have an incredible way of describing things.
This piece makes me feel as if I'm right in the story.
Are you planning to be a professional author someday?
I couldn't help but cry when I read your story.
How in the world do you come up with such good ideas?
Do you mind if I share this with another teacher?
I must let the principal see what a gifted writer you are.
I can hardly wait to see what you'll write next.
It's kids like you that make me glad I'm a teacher.
I wouldn't have missed reading this for anything in the world.
Thank you for sharing this wonderful piece with me.
This is what makes me glad to be a writing teacher.
Wow! Could you teach everyone else in the class to do this?
Your writing experience is really beginning to pay off.
I don't know if anyone else could have done the job you've done.
Think of the possibilities of what you could do with this!
When I read your story I thought of one word: INCREDIBLE!.
This story is going to be really popular with the other kids.
I like the way you make me know your characters.
I like the way you try, even when you hit a snag.
A publisher would LOVE a piece like this.
This is exactly what I've been looking for.
This is what great writing looks like.

You have a great sense of humor.
You have such a way with words.
Do you know how funny you are?

You've written from a fresh angle.
Who taught you to write like this?
You had better get ready for fame!

Now *this* is a jewel!
What is your secret?
I LOVE IT! I LOVE IT!

LAGNIAPPE
A Little Something Extra

Teaching children to write is like letting a genie out of a bottle: rewarding, exhilarating, fascinating, enlightening, and more than a little terrifying. With the genie's release, however, comes a torrent of creativity and the mastery of life-enhancing skills. The resulting writing explosion is phenomenal.

The Writing Menu has been written to help you create a nurturing writing environment within your classroom, to challenge young authors, and to facilitate writing across the curriculum. Helping a student unlock the key to self-expression enhances his future educational and job opportunities.

To improve the life of a child is a beautiful thing.

- Notes -

Index

Resources

Burchers, Sam, Max, & Bryan. *Vocabulary Cartoons: Building An Educated Vocabulary With Visual Mnemonics.* Punta Gorda, FL: New Monic Books: 1998.

Fiderer, Adele. *Teaching Writing: A Workshop Approach.* New York, NY: Scholastic Professional Books, 1993.

Forney, Melissa. *Dynamite Writing Ideas.* Gainesville, FL: Maupin House Publishing, 1996.

Freeman, Marcia. *Teaching the Youngest Writers.* Gainesville, FL: Maupin House Publishing, 1998.

Hablitzel, Marie & Stitzer, Kim. *Draw*Write*Now*, Books One through Six. Poulsbo, WA: Barker Creek Publishing, 1997.

Hannaford, Carla. *The Dominance Factor: How Knowing Your Dominant Eye, Ear, Brain, Hand, and Foot Can Improve Your Learning.* Arlington, VA: Great Ocean Publishers, 1997.

Heller, Ruth. *Many Luscious Lollipops: A Book About Adjectives.* New York, NY: Grosset and Dunlap, 1989.

Lewis, Valerie & Mayles, Walter. *Best Books for Children.* New York, NY: Avon Books, 1998.

Loftus, Diana Standing & Thompson, Kimberly. *Art Connection: Integrating Art Throughout the Curriculum.* Glenview, IL: Goodyear Books, 1995.

Mandel Family. *Cyberspace for Kids. 600 Sites That Are Kid-Tested and Parent-Approved*, Grades 7 & 8. Grand Rapids, MI: Instructional Fair, 1999.

Rothlein, Liz & Meinbach, Anita Meyer. *Using Children's Books in the Classroom.* Glenview, IL: Scott Foresman & Co., 1991.

Russell, William F. *Family Learning.* St. Charles, IL: First Word, 1997.

SCBE Multiple Intelligence Homepage, http://www.scbe.on.ca/mit/mi.htm

School Smart Kids Newsletter, http://www.howtolearn.com/ndil3.html

Spinelli, Eileen. *Somebody Loves You, Mr. Hatch.* New York: Simon & Schuster Books for Young Readers, 1991.

Tobias, Cynthia Ulrich. *The Way They Learn.* Wheaton, IL: Tyndale, 1994.

WWW.Alphasmart.com